UNDERSTANDING THE CONTESTED AUCTION

Nowadays good opponents are unlikely to leave the auction to you just because you hold the majority of high cards. Many auctions are contested, leaving you with far less bidding space and, consequently, many more undiscussed sequences.

Understanding the Contested Auction shows you how to understand the principles that will guide you through the maze of competitive bidding, and demonstrates how you can inconvenience your opponents should they have the balance of strength.

This is a brilliant and perceptive contribution to bridge from two outstandingly successful writers, players and teachers.

UNDERSTANDING THE CONTESTED AUCTION

Ron Klinger &
Andrew Kambites

CASSELL&CO
IN ASSOCIATION WITH
PETER CRAWLEY

Published in Great Britain 2001
in association with Peter Crawley
by Cassell & Co
Wellington House, 125 Strand, London WC2R 0BB
a member of the Orion Publishing Group

A catalogue record for this book is available from the
British Library

ISBN 0–304–35780–4

Typeset by Modern Bridge Publications
P.O. Box 140, Northbridge NSW 1560 Australia
Printed in Great Britain by Mackays of Chatham, Kent

Contents

INTRODUCTION

Why do so many bridge players achieve a competent standard but fail to improve further? We suggest that it might be that while learning appropriate point counts for bids, and rules for cards, these players do not really achieve understanding.

If you can understand why a particular bid shows a certain type of hand, it removes the strain of having to commit lots of seemingly unrelated facts to your memory. If you can understand the principles of bidding, you can then apply them to unfamiliar situations and be confident that you and your partner are on the same wavelength.

Understanding the Contested Auction examines the principles that govern competitive bidding. We believe that the ideas presented should be both easy to absorb and profitable to apply. By the end you will have acquired the greatest single gift that can be bestowed upon a bridge player, the gift of good judgement.

Ron Klinger
Andrew Kambites
2001

Chapter 1

The Offence to Defence Ratio

Where should a book on competitive bidding begin? It is more important to understand the essential principles than to plough through endless examples and hope to learn them all. After understanding comes the ability to make your own decisions. Some simple but very important principles can be demonstrated by these hands:

(a) ♠ A 9 3   ♡ A Q 3 2   ◇ A 7 4   ♣ 9 4 3

(b) ♠ K Q J 10 9 8   ♡ 8   ◇ 9 7 4   ♣ 7 4 3

With (a) you would happily open 1NT, 12-14, yet if your right-hand opponent opened the bidding, you should definitely pass, whether the opening was 1NT or a suit bid.

With (b) an opening bid of 1♠ would be ill-judged. Admittedly you have good playing strength but you have only six high card points and your defensive strength is close to zero. What if partner took your opening bid seriously and doubled an enemy contract? If you run back to spades, you might concede a sizable penalty and if you pass, your lack of defence may see their contract roll home.

You might consider opening with a pre-emptive 3♠, a bid which promises little in the way of defence, but even not vulnerable, your playing strength is below expectancy. If your methods include weak two bids, then a 2♠ opening falls within the normal range for this action. Otherwise, you should refrain from opening with a hand such as this. Even so, if right-hand opponent (RHO) opened 1♡, you should have few reservations about overcalling 1♠ despite your modest high card values.

So, with (a) you would open but not overcall, while with (b) you would not open but an overcall is sane. What is the fundamental difference between these two hands?

(a) ♠ A 9 3   ♡ A Q 3 2   ◇ A 7 4   ♣ 9 4 3

(b) ♠ K Q J 10 9 8   ♡ 8   ◇ 9 7 4   ♣ 7 4 3

With (a) you have three or four tricks either as declarer or in defence (especially if they choose a heart contract). That is not to say you should pass as dealer. Game, or more, for your side could be laydown. However if an opponent opens the bidding, there is no burning desire to enter the auction in order to seek your side's best denomination. As hand (a) is as useful in defence as in offence, it is said to have a very low 'Offence to Defence Ratio' (ODR).

Hand (b) has plenty of playing strength as long as spades are trumps. If spades are not trumps, it might turn out to be useless. Hand (b) has a very high ODR.

In any contested auction, the higher the ODR of your hand, the more important it is to enter the auction.

Let's look at more hands to derive the relevant guidelines. Suppose at game all RHO opened 1♡. Would you overcall or pass with these hands, which have the same high card point count?

(c) ♠ A 8 7 3 2   ♡ Q 5 3   ◇ A 4 3   ♣ Q 2

(d) ♠ K Q J 10 9   ♡ 8 4 3   ◇ A 4 3   ♣ Q 2

Firstly, consider the spades. In (c) the ace is likely to take one trick either offensively (in your spade contract) or defensively (against any contract they play). The ace is thus (probably) equally valuable in offence and defence. When a card is neither predominantly offensive or predominantly defensive, it is said to be 'neutral'.

Your spade holding in (d) is very offensive, certain to make four tricks if spades are trumps but probably worth no more than one or at best two tricks against their suit contract. Similarly, the ◇A is as likely to take a trick in offence as in defence.

In your side's long suits, aces are neutral but queens and jacks are offensive values.

Now, take a look at the other suits. In (c) the $\heartsuit$Q may make a trick against their heart contract but it will not surprise anyone if it is worthless if you play in spades, particularly if dummy has two hearts as well. Likewise, the ♣Q is at least as likely to score a trick in defence as in offence. To see why, consider these layouts:

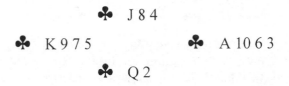

♣ 9 8 4

♣ K J 7 5   ♣ A 10 6 3

♣ Q 2

If East-West are playing the hand, they may have to guess who has the ♣Q. If North-South are playing in spades, it is hard to see any rational defensive play which could give declarer a club trick.

♣ J 8 4

♣ K 9 7 5   ♣ A 10 6 3

♣ Q 2

If East-West are playing the hand, they have a club to lose (as long as neither opponent leads a club). If North-South are playing in spades, they have the same two club losers that they would have if they had no club honour at all. Declarer cannot even set up a trick in clubs (to discard a loser elsewhere) as long as the defenders are passive and do not lead a club.

In your side's short suits (the opponents' long suits), aces are still neutral but queens and jacks are likely to be defensive (the reverse of the situation for queens and jacks in your side's long suits).

The greater your ODR, the more you should strive to compete further. The lower your ODR, the more inclined you should be to defend.

Hand (c) has a very low ODR. There is little enthusiasm to overcall their 1$\heartsuit$ with 1♠. Hand (d) has a far more promising ODR. You should overcall 1♠ at any vulnerability.

Suppose the bidding has started:

West	North	East	South
No	No	3♡	?

What action would you take with these hands?

(e) ♠ A Q 9 6 3   ♡ 8   ◇ A 10 9 8 4   ♣ 8 4

(f) ♠ A Q 9 6 3   ♡ 8 2   ◇ A 10 9   ♣ 9 8 4

Assuming your methods do not include a bid to show both your suits at once with (e), the choice is between 3♠ and passing.

If you do bid 3♠ and partner has support, partner will raise with three tricks or better and will pass with fewer than three potential tricks. Imagine partner has a sound hand with three tricks, such as:

♠ K 10 2   ♡ 9 7 5 4   ◇ K 6   ♣ A 7 3

If you hold (e) 4♠ is a strong favourite to make but with (f), 4♠ has no play. The more shapely (e) has far more offensive potential than the balanced (f). While both hands appear to have roughly equal defensive potential against a heart contract, (f) has greater potential because not only are your ◇A and partner's ◇K more likely to score but you also have prospects of a diamond ruff. Hand (e) has much greater ODR than (f) and so makes a far better overcall of 3♠.

The more unbalanced your hand, the greater your ODR.

Finally, suppose the bidding has been:

West	North	East	South
1♠	3♡	?	

3♡ is described as an intermediate jump-overcall showing a sound opening bid with a good 6-card heart suit. What action would you take, at game all, with these hands:

(g) ♠ Q 7 4 3   ♡ 9 8   ◇ K 8 5 4   ♣ Q 6 3

(h) ♠ Q 7 4 3   ♡ 9 8   ◇ K Q 6 4   ♣ 9 6 3

With just seven high card points and a doubleton, you would be stretching if you bid 3♠, but equally you really want to show partner that you have a spade fit. Should you bid 3♠?

Suppose partner's hand looks like this:

♠ A K 6 5 2   ♡ 10 7 2   ◇ A 3 2   ♣ 7 5

Opposite (g) partner has little chance in 3♠. You need West to hold the ♣A and ♣K and you would need to drive out both these honours before the defenders establish a diamond trick. If West starts by cashing a couple of hearts, the danger of a diamond discard will be obvious if West has both top clubs. It will be an easy matter to switch to a diamond at trick 3. What if you let West play in hearts? You might be able to defeat 3♡ with two spades, two diamonds and perhaps the ♣Q.

With (h) opposite, 3♠ is almost laydown (losing two hearts and two clubs), while you would be lucky indeed to score the two spades and three diamond tricks needed to defeat 3♡. Clearly (h) has better ODR than (g). Can you see why?

The more your high cards reinforce each other in the same suit, the higher your ODR. Combined honours increase your ODR. The same honours divided among two or more suits reduce your ODR.

This can be seen easily enough in an uncontested auction when you are interested only in considering your offensive strength. A hand is stronger if the honours are concentrated in the same suit because then they help each other to build tricks.

♠ K 8 6 ♡ Q 6 5	♠ K Q 6 ♡ 7 6 5
opposite	opposite
♠ 4 3 2 ♡ 4 3 2	♠ 4 3 2 ♡ 4 3 2
You may make no tricks at all here.	One spade trick is sure and two are possible if the ♠A is onside.

Chapter 2

The Law of Total Tricks

Once in a blue moon an idea sweeps through the bridge world and revolutionises thinking. The so-called *Law of Total Tricks* is so accurate in assessing potential in the contested auction and so easy to use that it is being introduced early and used to justify many subsequent bidding decisions. You will find the 'law' discussed in other books of ours but it is worth emphasising it once more. It is exceedingly difficult to acquire good judgement in competitive bidding without understanding the 'law'.

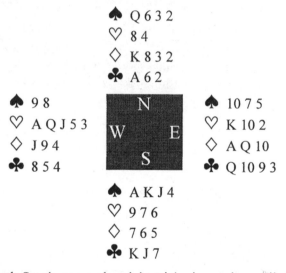

♠ Q 6 3 2
♡ 8 4
◇ K 8 3 2
♣ A 6 2

♠ 9 8   ♠ 10 7 5
♡ A Q J 5 3   ♡ K 10 2
◇ J 9 4   ◇ A Q 10
♣ 8 5 4   ♣ Q 10 9 3

♠ A K J 4
♡ 9 7 6
◇ 7 6 5
♣ K J 7

North-South can make eight tricks in spades while East-West can make eight tricks in hearts. Adding these, the total is 16, in other words, '16 TOTAL TRICKS'. North-South have eight trumps for their spade contract, while East-West have eight trumps for a heart contract. We say there are '16 TOTAL TRUMPS'.

The Law of Total Tricks states that the number of total tricks will generally equal the number of total trumps.

This is a reasonably typical part-score deal. Each side has an 8-card fit and the points are almost equally divided. The diamond finesse works for East-West while the club finesse works for North-South. Note the implications. If North-South allow East-West to play in 2♡, they can expect a very poor score. North-South should compete to 2♠ but would be unwise to push to 3♠ if East-West bid 3♡.

East-West do best to bid 3♡ over 2♠. That will fail, but the loss in 3♡ figures to be less than defending 2♠. Here 'absolute par' (the term given to the contract when neither side can improve its score by bidding higher), at love all, is 3♡ doubled for one down. As North-South are hardly likely to double for one off, because of the drastic consequences if wrong, particularly at teams scoring, it is sound strategy even when vulnerable for East-West to bid 3♡ over 2♠. The difference between -100 and -110, significant at pairs, is of no consequence at teams but it may goad North-South into bidding 3♠. Then you score plus for defeating 3♠ instead of minus defending 2♠.

With a slight change in the layout, giving South the ◇K, the diamond finesse now works for North-South and fails for East-West.

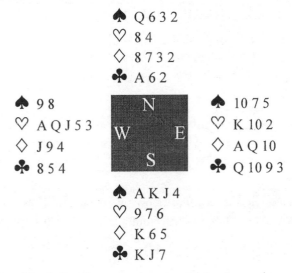

$$
\begin{array}{c}
\spadesuit\ Q\,6\,3\,2 \\
\heartsuit\ 8\,4 \\
\diamondsuit\ 8\,7\,3\,2 \\
\clubsuit\ A\,6\,2
\end{array}
$$

West: ♠ 9 8 ♡ A Q J 5 3 ◇ J 9 4 ♣ 8 5 4

East: ♠ 10 7 5 ♡ K 10 2 ◇ A Q 10 ♣ Q 10 9 3

South: ♠ A K J 4 ♡ 9 7 6 ◇ K 6 5 ♣ K J 7

Now North-South can make nine tricks in spades, while East-West make only seven tricks in hearts. Nevertheless, the number of total tricks (16) has not changed and still equals the total number of trumps.

There are many implications of the LTT. The following guide-lines assume that both you and your opponents have found a fit and that you are in a position to estimate the total trumps. In practice it is usually not too difficult to calculate the total trumps. The number of trumps your side holds is often clearly revealed and from the bidding to date, it is usually possible to make a sensible assessment of the number of trumps held by the opponents. There is often a close relationship between the two, which is examined further in Chapter 9.

It is always correct to bid on if the LTT suggests that both contracts might make.

As a practical application for part-score hands, if the points are roughly equal between the two sides:

1. With 16 total trumps it is correct to bid 2-over-2, e.g., 2♠ over 2♡.

2. With 17 total trumps it is correct to bid 3-over-2, e.g. 3♢ over 2♠.

3. With 18 total trumps it is correct to bid 3-over-3, e.g. 3♠ over 3♢.

It is usually correct to bid on if the LTT suggests that one contract may make while the other may fail.

4. With 16 total trumps it is almost always correct to bid 3-over-their-2, e.g., 3♡ over their 2♠.

5. With 17 total trumps it is usually correct to bid 3-over-their-3, e.g., 3♠ over their 3♡.

In the last two cases, the advice is rather more cautious as the recommended strategy is not always correct. Be a touch careful when vulnerable at pairs when playing against enterprising opponents, who might chance a double for +200.

At the part-score level it is rarely correct to bid on if the LTT suggests that both contracts might fail.

6. With 16 total trumps it is usually poor strategy to bid 3-over-3, e.g., 3♡ over their 3♣. If you can make 3♡ (9 tricks), they figure to be two down in 3♣ (7 tricks), and vice versa. Often both contracts will be one down (8 tricks apiece).

Let's look at how the LTT applies at higher contracts:

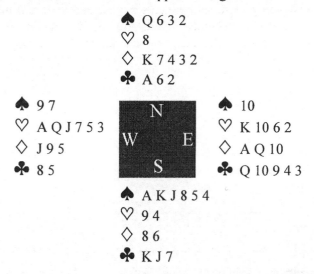

```
              ♠ Q 6 3 2
              ♡ 8
              ◇ K 7 4 3 2
              ♣ A 6 2
♠ 9 7                        ♠ 10
♡ A Q J 7 5 3       N        ♡ K 10 6 2
◇ J 9 5         W       E    ◇ A Q 10
♣ 8 5               S        ♣ Q 10 9 4 3
              ♠ A K J 8 5 4
              ♡ 9 4
              ◇ 8 6
              ♣ K J 7
```

North-South can make 4♠ and East-West can make 4♡. Par is 5♡ doubled, one down. Note that North-South have ten spades and East-West have ten hearts. 20 total trumps and 20 total tricks. Bingo!

The LTT is not quite so easy to apply at these higher levels. For a start, the number of trumps held by the opponents may not be as clear. In addition, short suits, in particular voids, will add to the total number of tricks without any necessity for extra trumps.

What if you believe there are 18 total trumps and you must decide whether to continue to 4♠ over 4♡? Suppose they are vulnerable and you are not. Let's assume, for simplicity, that a contract will be doubled only if it is due to go at least two off.

(1) If 4♡ and 4♠ are both one off, bidding 4♠ turns +100 into -50.

(2) If 4♡ is on and 4♠ two off, then bidding 4♠ turns -620 into -300.

(3) If 4♡ is two off (and you are in a position to double it) and 4♠ is making, then bidding on turns +500 into +420.

The most probable of these scenarios is (1), but when it is right to bid on, especially at teams, it tends to be very right, as in (2).

17

The calculations are complicated by the fact that when you bid on, the opponents may misjudge and bid too high. Thus, if the situation is (2), they might be reluctant to settle for a modest penalty and bid to a doomed 5♥. Now bidding 4♠ has turned -620 into +100.

Clearly at the higher levels it is sometimes winning bridge to bid on even if both contracts might fail by one trick. This type of decision will be examined in more detail in Chapter 12.

Some more useful guide-lines:

Compete to the level equal to the number of trumps held by your side. If feasible in your methods, try to reach this level as quickly as possible when you have a weakish hand.

Try not to let the opponents play at a trick-level equal to their number of trumps.

These guide-lines, particularly the last one, are particularly relevant in Chapter 9, which covers protective bidding.

So does the LTT always work? Please remember that, despite its excellence, it is only an approximation, which will be right most of the time, but not all of the time. Take a look at this layout, which is an adaptation from the earlier example on page 14.

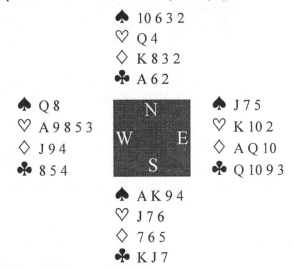

There are still 16 total trumps but now North-South can make only seven tricks in spades and East-West make the same number of tricks in hearts. Why is this?

If you look at the major suit holdings, you will see that each side has a queen and a jack in the opponents' trump suit. This change has significantly lowered the ODR of the hand. If players can recognise this lower ODR, then they can judge that there may well be fewer total tricks than total trumps. They should thus be less keen to enter a competitive auction or to try to outbid their opponents once a competitive auction has developed.

Likewise if players have hands with a high ODR, there might be more total tricks than trumps. For example:

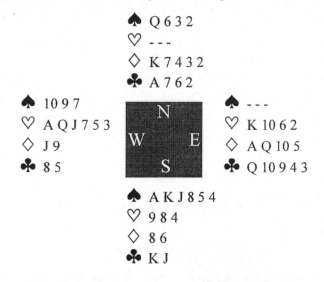

♠ Q 6 3 2
♡ - - -
◇ K 7 4 3 2
♣ A 7 6 2

♠ 10 9 7
♡ A Q J 7 5 3
◇ J 9
♣ 8 5

♠ - - -
♡ K 10 6 2
◇ A Q 10 5
♣ Q 10 9 4 3

♠ A K J 8 5 4
♡ 9 8 4
◇ 8 6
♣ K J

A void in the opponents' long suit increases the ODR. Be prepared to bid one more than usual with this asset. Here total trumps are 20, but on best play, best defence, there are 22 total tricks. Par is 6♡ doubled one down.

Chapter 3

Overcalling a Suit with a Suit

When you make an opening bid, you start a discussion. Most of the time partner will respond and if the opponents are kind enough to keep silent, you can sensibly develop your hand description with your rebid.

An overcall also makes a statement but the chance for a fruitful dialogue is greatly reduced. The overcall needs to be as clear a statement as feasible since it may well be the only opportunity you have. Overcaller's partner (called 'the advancer') is less likely to take any action. It needs to be a special 6-7 points for advancer to bid if support for your suit is not held. Even when the advancer does bid, the opponents may have pushed the bidding to a very high level before you have another chance. A constructive dialogue by the overcalling side is a rare privilege.

There are many different styles of overcalling. While each has its merits and shortcomings, and one need not dismiss other styles out of hand, there are a number of tests that you can apply to help decide whether or not to overcall.

Suppose RHO opens 1♡ at love all. Should you overcall 1♠ with:

♠ J 8 7 4 3   ♡ K Q 10   ◇ Q 9   ♣ Q 4 2

Firstly, imagine that you do overcall 1♠ and LHO jumps to 4♡. Partner now bids 4♠ and RHO doubles. How do you feel?

Quite ill, we imagine. The bird of happiness is not about to alight on your shoulders. No doubt partner is looking at a singleton heart, imagining that will be good news for you. It won't! Indeed, it is not difficult to see that you might lose 500 when you might have defeated 4♡ without any great feat in defence.

To quantify your malaise is not difficult. Your hand simply has too low an ODR to justify an overcall.

Secondly, suppose you do overcall 1♠ and LHO finishes in 3NT. Partner starts with the ♠K. Do you feel the defence has a flying start?

It is all too likely that partner's ♠K lead is from ♠K-x and declarer may now have not just two but perhaps three tricks in spades. Your minor suit queens are unlikely to be entries. If need be, declarer will first drive out your heart stoppers and then take any minor suit finesses into the safe hand.

A sound overcall has a high ODR and indicates a good lead to partner. The first example falls short on both counts and a pass is strongly urged. Here are two more hands. At game all RHO opens 1♣. Would you overcall 1♠ with these hands?

(a) ♠ A K Q 10   ♡ 8 6   ◇ 8 3 2   ♣ 8 5 3 2

(b) ♠ A 8 5 4 2   ♡ A Q   ◇ K Q 4 2   ♣ 9 8

With (a) the ODR is not very high. The shape is balanced and because you have only a 4-card suit, you may have two or three defensive tricks. If you overcall 1♠ and partner sacrifices in 4♠, things may not go as well as partner had hoped (although if partner has five trumps and an unbalanced hand, 4♠ may be a fine spot). Despite the drawbacks, there are two reasons why you should bid 1♠.

Firstly, you desperately want a spade lead. This alone justifies the overcall. Not only might your spade winners vanish if you do not take them quickly but if partner chooses to lead away from an honour in some other suit, that figures to cost a trick as well.

Secondly, a 1♠ overcall takes away their bidding space. In particular, you have prevented a 1♡ response and they might find it hard to uncover a heart fit unless they play negative doubles.

How about (b)? The ODR is low but the 5-2-4-2 pattern is certainly more promising for offence than a 5-3-3-2 would be. Naturally you should be reluctant to pass with 15 points. Partner could have a balanced 9-10 points, enough to make game a strong prospect, and find it hard to rake up a bid, even in the balancing seat. While a vulnerable overcall with a poor suit is undesirable, there is more danger in passing than in overcalling 1♠.

Advancer replies to an overcall

An overcall at the one level has historically shown about 8-15 HCP and normally at least a 5-card suit. Advancer would consider three trumps as adequate support but might have more than one reason to raise partner's suit.

Suppose the bidding has been:

South	West	North	East
1♡	1♠	No	?

What action would you take as East with these hands?

(c) ♠ Q 8 3	(d) ♠ K 8 3	(e) ♠ K 8 3
♡ 9 7	♡ 9 7	♡ K 7
◇ K 7 4 3	◇ A K 8 3	◇ A K 8 3
♣ 9 6 5 3	♣ 9 6 5 3	♣ 9 6 5 3

With (c) East can be confident that chances for game East-West are remote opposite a simple overcall. South figures to be quite strong and North-South probably have at least an 8-card fit in hearts. Hoping to subject South to a little pressure, East can raise to 2♠. This single raise opposite an overcall does not show significant high card values. It is as much pre-emptive as constructive. If partner has a weak hand, there is little chance that the opponents will let you play 2♠ anyway.

With (d) East is worth a mild game try. Opposite a maximum overcall, the spade game might be a good proposition. Clearly East cannot bid 2♠ for each of these conflicting purposes, pre-emption vs a game try. The popular style is to play the direct raise of an overcall as primarily pre-emptive, hand (c), while with (d) advancer bids the opponents' suit, here 2♡, to show a hand worth a game try. This action by advancer is called an 'unassuming cue bid'.

To reject the game try, West repeats the suit at the cheapest level, here 2♠. If South passes, any rebid by West beyond 2♠ should be played as forcing to game. If South bids beyond East's 2♡, pass by West shows a minimum overcall, no interest in game, while 3♠ over a three-level bid by South should be taken as competitive, not forcing.

With (e) East wants to make a strong game try. East again starts with an unassuming cue bid (2♡) but now if West rebids 2♠, rejection, East will make one more effort with a raise to 3♠ to try to inspire West into action.

Note the difference in these sequences:

South	West	North	East	South	West	North	East
1♡	1♠	No	2♡	1♡	1♠	No	3♡...
No	2♠	No	3♠ ...	The jump-cue-bid shows extra
East has a strong raise with	trumps. East has the same strong
three trumps.	raise but with four trumps.

What should East do with these cards?

♠ K 8 3 2   ♡ 9 7   ◇ J 10 9 3   ♣ 9 6 5

The modern style is to treat all direct raises of an overcall as pre-emptive. Raise to two pre-emptively with three trumps, and to three with four trumps. Accordingly, East should jump to 3♠. This shows a poor hand but promises four trumps and a high ODR. The actual hand has virtually no defence and the 4-card support reduces the defensive potential of West's spade holding.

It may seem dangerous to jump to 3♠ with such a motley collection but with at least a 9-card fit the LTT suggests that you should compete to the three-level. If you can do so before your opponents can get their act together, so much the better.

Once you know your own fit, you can estimate their fit. When you have a 10-card fit, they have only 3 cards in your suit and 23 cards in the other three suits. With two 7-card fits, they must hold nine cards in the remaining suit. With one 7-card fit, they can have two 8-card fits in the other suits. Thus, you can deduce that if your side has ten trumps, then they will have at least a 9-card fit or two 8-card fits.

Likewise, if you have a 9-card spade fit, as above, the opponents have only four spades. They have 22 other cards and so are bound to have at least an 8-card fit (with two 7-card fits). In practice, when you have a 9-card fit, chances are high that they also have at least a 9-card fit.

If you have an 8-card fit, they have 21 cards outside. Unless they have three 7-card fits (less than a 20% chance), they have an 8-card fit, too.

With 4+ support for partner's overcall, it is winning bridge to raise aggressively, but with a misfit it pays to be conservative.

Suppose the bidding has started:

South	West	North	East
1♣	1♠	No	?

What should East do with these cards?

(f)   ♠ 9   ♡ K 5 4 2   ◇ J 9 5 4   ♣ K 9 6 3

(g)   ♠ 9   ♡ K 5 4 2   ◇ A 9 5 4   ♣ K J 6 3

(h)   ♠ 9   ♡ K 5 4 2   ◇ A Q 5 4   ♣ K J 6 3

These hands are far more suitable for defence than as a dummy to partner's spade contract. Because a 1♠ overcall can be made with as few as 8 HCP, a no-trump bid by advancer should be somewhat stronger than would be applicable opposite an opening bid.

With (f), East passes.
With (g), East bids 1NT, showing around 8-11 points.
With (h), East bids 2NT, showing around 12-14 points.

If all this seems ultra-cautious, remember that in no-trumps, you must develop tricks. With no source of tricks, you will probably need to turn to partner's spade suit. With no help in spades, this may be difficult since your shortage may make entries to partner's hand a problem.

What if you want to bid your own suit as advancer?

South	West	North	East
1♣	1♠	No	?

What should East do with these cards?

(i)   ♠ 9   ♡ A J 10 4 3 2   ◇ Q 6 2   ♣ 9 4 3

(j)   ♠ Q 2   ♡ A J 10 4 3 2   ◇ A K 8   ♣ 8 4

(k)   ♠ J 2   ♡ A J 7 4 3   ◇ A K 8   ♣ 8 4 3

Traditionally a change of suit was constructive but non-forcing. Nowadays most strong players prefer to play advancer's new suit as forcing and we would endorse this approach. In that case, East is forced to pass with (i), which is too weak for a two-level change of suit. However, if South re-opens with a double and North passes for penalties, East should definitely run to 2♡.

The advantage of playing 2♡ as forcing here can be seen in hands (j) and (k) which merit a serious game try. With (j), 2♡ preserves space for further action later. If partner rebids 2♠, you can try again with 3♡, hoping to hear 3NT or secondary heart support. If partner raises to 4♡, you will revert to 4♠.

With (k), East is also worth 2♡. The suit is modest but bidding it is the only probable chance of locating a 5-3 heart fit. If West cannot support hearts and has a weak hand, the most likely rebid will be 2♠, which East would pass.

Once you adopt change-of-suit by advancer as forcing, you do not need to jump-shift or jump to game to show a strong, single-suited hand. A bid of 3♡ here is best played as a Fit-Jump, showing a good heart suit plus support for spades (see Chapter 13) while a double-jump to 4♡ can be used as a Splinter Bid, showing a strong raise to 4♠ together with a singleton or void in hearts.

After a two-level overcall, the same principles apply for advancer. While 10 HCP and a strong suit justify a two-level overcall, advancer should play partner to have opening values. The long, strong suit compensates for a slight shortfall in HCP. A fit with partner's minor suit is a great advantage for no-trumps since it will help to establish the suit.

South	West	North	East
1♡	2♣	No	?

What should East do with these cards?

(l)   ♠ 8 4 3   ♡ A 10 7 3   ◇ A 6 3   ♣ J 10 8

(m)   ♠ 10 4 3   ♡ A 10 7 3   ◇ A K 3   ♣ J 10 8

(n)   ♠ A J 8 3   ♡ K 7 5 2   ◇ K Q J 6   ♣ 9

South	West	North	East
1♡	2♣	No	?

(l)　　♠ 8 4 3　　♡ A 10 7 3　　◇ A 6 3　　♣ J 10 8

Hand (l) has only nine points but is well worth 2NT. It is easy to imagine winning the opening lead with the ♡A and running a lot of clubs tricks next. Any club finesse you need to take is likely to work, as it will be through the opening bidder.

(m)　　♠ 10 4 3　　♡ A 10 7 3　　◇ A K 3　　♣ J 10 8

Similarly, hand (m) is worth 3NT because of the extra diamond trick. Do we hear you cry, 'What about the spades?' Once the opponents have bid a suit, you need to worry about that suit. Even if it is possible for them to take five spade tricks, it is not likely that South will lead a spade.

(n)　　♠ A J 8 3　　♡ K 7 5 2　　◇ K Q J 6　　♣ 9

Hand (n) is worth only 2NT for all its 14 HCP. The drawbacks include lack of a fit for clubs, the absence of a second stopper in hearts and the possible need to give up the lead to establish some diamond tricks. This hand may play very badly in no-trumps if the ♡K is the only stopper in hearts and is forced out early unless you have nine running tricks. With as much as the ◇A and ♣A-K-Q-x-x, partner will give you 3NT.

South	West	North	East
1♠	2♡	No	?

What should East do with these cards?

(o)　　♠ 9 6 5 2　　♡ K 10 7 3 2　　◇ Q J 2　　♣ 4

(p)　　♠ 9 6 5 2　　♡ A 10 7 3　　◇ A K J　　♣ 8 5

With hand (o) jump to 4♡ to show strong support but poor defence, a high ODR. The LTT tells you to bid for ten tricks with a 10-card fit.

With hand (p) bid 2♠. You also plan to reach 4♡ but this route suggests defensive strength outside hearts and a lower ODR.

Jump-Overcalls in a suit

Subject to system agreement there are three basic hand types for a jump-overcall of 2♠:

(q) ♠ A Q J 7 4 3   ♡ A 8 4   ◇ A 8   ♣ 8 3

(r) ♠ A Q J 7 4 3   ♡ A 8 4   ◇ 9 8   ♣ 8 3

(s) ♠ A Q J 7 4 3   ♡ 9 8 4   ◇ 9 8   ♣ 8 3

Hand (q) is a Strong Jump-Overcall, a hand which in an uncontested auction would be opened 1♠ with a jump-rebid to 3♠ in mind.

Hand (r) is an Intermediate Jump-Overcall, a minimum opening bid with a 6-card suit. The Intermediate Jump reflects the sort of hand which one would open 1♠ and rebid 2♠ over 1NT.

Hand (s) is a Weak Jump-Overcall and shows the type of hand which would be suitable for a weak two-opening.

Traditionally, jump-overcalls were played as strong but the powerful, single-suited hand can be introduced in a competitive auction by starting with a takeout double and bidding the long suit on the next round.

A sensible approach is to play jump-overcalls 'according to vulnerability' (ATV), so that they are strong at red (only your side is vulnerable), intermediate at equal (both sides vulnerable or both sides not vulnerable) and weak at green (the opponents are vulnerable, you are not). It is also popular to play jump-overcalls as 'weak throughout' but naturally when vulnerable, the playing strength and suit quality will compensate for the deficiency in high card values.

Pushing the opponents about at green vulnerability is sound tactics. Indeed, if partner has passed and right-hand opponent opens, you are unlikely to come to much harm if you make a weak jump-overcall in a good five-card suit.

Chapter 4

Opener's Partner Bids after an Overcall

If the overcall has not prevented you from making the bid you intended, then go ahead and make it anyway. When the overcall prevents that, you may have a hard decision.

Responder likes partner's suit

South	West	North	East
1♠	2♡	?	

What should North do with these cards?

(a) ♠ Q J 4 3   ♡ 9 4   ◇ 9 8 5 4   ♣ 9 3 2

(b) ♠ 10 9 4 3   ♡ Q 4   ◇ 9 8 5 4   ♣ J 3 2

(c) ♠ K 9 8   ♡ 8 3   ◇ K 7 3 2   ♣ 9 4 3 2

(d) ♠ K 9 8   ♡ 8 3 2   ◇ K 7 3 2   ♣ 9 4 3

If you want to support spades, there is nothing to prevent your making the raise you would have made without the overcall, but the borderline cases are of interest.

Generally, with decent support for opener, it is reasonable to overbid by up to a trick if the alternative is to pass and leave partner unaware of the degree of fit. With (a) and (b) you would have passed 1♠ unless your methods include a pre-emptive jump-raise to show fewer than 6 HCP. Over 2♡ you have the choice of passing, leaving partner in the dark about your 4-card support, or overbidding with 2♠.

Hand (a) has a high ODR, making 2♠ attractive. Hand (b) has a queen and a jack in the short suits and a lower ODR. Pass is recommended, unless you play pre-emptive jump-raises. [Some play 3♠ here shows a pre-emptive raise, 2♠ a normal raise and 3♡, the enemy suit, is a limit raise or better. They would bid 3♠ on both (a) and (b).]

With hand (c) you would have been happy to bid 2♠ without the overcall and so there is no problem in bidding 2♠ now.

How about hand (d)? Without the overcall, you would respond 1NT, given the flat shape. As that option no longer exists, should you pass or bid 2♠? The answer is emphatic: show the support. This may help partner if the auction becomes competitive, such as LHO jumping to 4♡.

A jump-overcall by RHO may cause you even greater problems. Suppose at red vulnerability, partner opens 1♠ and RHO bids 3♡, an intermediate jump-overcall. What action would you take with these:

(e) ♠ Q J 4 3   ♡ 8 5   ◇ K Q 10 4 ♣ 7 3 2

(f) ♠ 8 4 3 2   ♡ K J   ◇ Q 7 3 2   ♣ Q 5 3

(g) ♠ Q J 4 3   ♡ 8 5   ◇ K Q 10 4 ♣ K 3 2

Hand (e) has a high ODR. You should definitely bid 3♠.

Hand (f) has a poor ODR. It is better to pass.

How about hand (g)? It is a strong raise to 3♠ but how can you expect partner to judge whether to go on to 4♠ if you could have hand (e) or hand (g) for a 3♠ bid? As opener should allow a little leeway for responder's support after an intervening bid, you should take the pressure off opener by bidding 4♠ yourself. A bid of 4♡ here would be a very strong raise to 4♠ and invite slam if opener has significantly better than a minimum opening.

The Negative Double

South	West	North	East
1♣	1♠	Double	

In the early days of bridge, North's double was for penalties. Today responder's low-level doubles of a suit bid are played for takeout and are called negative doubles. To pick up a hand strong enough in their suit to warrant playing penalties is rare. More pressing is the need to compete effectively in a suit which their bid has bypassed.

The primary focus for any negative double is any unbid major.

South	West	North	East	
1♣	1♠	Double		North is showing four hearts. North might have five hearts in a hand not strong enough for 2♥.

South	West	North	East	
1♣	1♥	Double		North has four spades. Instead of doubling, a 1♠ response would show five spades.

South	West	North	East	
1♣	1♦	Double		North has four cards in each major. With only one 4-card major, bid it.

South	West	North	East
1♦	2♣	Double	

Traditionally this double has also shown at least 4-4 in the majors. However, it is more practical to use it to show a desire to compete with at least one 4-card major. With a powerful hand, enough for game, and one 4-card major, opener can bid their suit, here 3♣.

The higher the double, the greater the strength shown. If the double does not commit the partnership beyond the two-level, 5 HCP may do.

South	West	North	East
1♦	2♣	?	

What should North do with these cards?

(h)   ♠ Q J 4 3   ♥ Q 10 5 4   ◇ 8 5 4   ♣ 6 2

(i)   ♠ 8 3   ♥ K Q 7 3   ◇ Q 7 3 2   ♣ 9 3 2

(j)   ♠ 8 3   ♥ K Q 7 3   ◇ A 9 3 2   ♣ 9 3 2

(k)   ♠ K 7 3 2   ♥ A 10 7 4 3 2   ◇ 8   ♣ 7 3

With hand (h), be prepared to double. You intend to pass any rebid unless opener bids the enemy suit, 3♣. With hand (i), do not double. If opener rebids 2♠ you will have to rebid 3◇ suggesting a hand as strong as (j). With (k), double and remove a 2◇ rebid to 2♥. A change of suit by the negative doubler is played as non-forcing.

South	West	North	East
1♣	1♠	Double	No
?			

Opener's reply to a negative double is largely a matter of commonsense. What should South do with these cards after the above beginning?

(l)   ♠ J 3   ♡ K 10 5 4   ◇ A 8   ♣ K J 10 7 2

(m)   ♠ A 3   ♡ K 10 5 4   ◇ A 8   ♣ K J 10 7 2

(n)   ♠ 8 7 3 2   ♡ K Q 3   ◇ K 4   ♣ A Q J 6

(o)   ♠ 8 7 3 2   ♡ K 4   ◇ K Q 3   ♣ A Q J 6

With (l), bid 2♡. Had partner responded 1♡, you would have happily raised to two.

With (m), rebid 3♡, as you would have after a 1♡ response.

With (n), you would have been planning a 1♠ or 1NT rebid over 1♡. As 1NT is undesirable, the best bet is to improvise with 2♡.

With (o), you are well and truly stuck. The sane choices are 1NT with no stopper or 2♣ with only a four-card suit. Both carry significant risk but if partner is strong, a 2♣ rebid is less likely to lead to the wrong game.

Playing for Penalties

South	West	North	East
1♣	1♠	?	

What should North do with a hand suitable for a penalty double of spades? As loud or soft doubles are illegal, the standard approach is to pass in tempo. South has another call and is expected not to pass unless strong in spades (and thus knowing that North cannot have a hand suitable to penalise 1♠).

If North and East pass, South should almost always re-open with a double if short in spades (singleton or doubleton). With a void in their suit, playing for penalties at a low level is usually unsound and it is better to find a descriptive rebid than to double.

South	West	North	East
1◇	1♠	No	No
?			

What should South do with these cards after the above start?

(p)	♠ 9	♡ K J 7	◇ A 9 6 3 2	♣ A 7 3 2
(q)	♠ - - -	♡ 9 3	◇ K Q J 7 4 3	♣ K J 10 4 3
(r)	♠ - - -	♡ 6 3	◇ A K Q 7 4 3	♣ K J 10 4 3
(s)	♠ K Q 4	♡ A 8	◇ K 10 9 4 3	♣ K 9 6

With (p), South is minimum but should definitely double, for takeout. With a penalties hand, quite likely on South's values, North will pass. With other holdings, North will reply to the double.

With (q), South suspects North is looking for penalties but with poor defence, a void in their suit and a very high ODR, do not double. A 2♣ re-opening carries the message to partner about the nature of your hand.

With (r), North again is probably hoping for penalties but even though 1♠ doubled might be beaten, the high ODR indicates that declaring is more appealing than defending. With so much playing strength, only four losers, a jump to 3♣ is warranted.

With (s), South's spade holding strongly suggests North does not have a penalty double of spades. As the other explanation for North's pass is weakness, South should pass rather than overbid with 1NT.

Suppose the auction starts this way:

South	West	North	East
1◇	1♠	No	2♣
No	No	?	

Some play a change of suit reply to an overcall as non-forcing and so some Easts try to rescue partner before a takeout double is passed for penalties. Suppose North doubles. What would that mean?

Modern style is to treat North's double in this kind of auction as a penalty double of the first suit (spades). If weak, North would not have enough to produce a double now opposite a possibly minimum opener.

A new suit by responder is natural and forcing in standard methods. What do you call here if partner opens 1♦ and next player overcalls 1♠?

(t) ♠ 9 7   ♡ A J 9 6 5   ♦ 9 3   ♣ A Q 5 2

(u) ♠ 9 7   ♡ A J 9 6 5 4   ♦ 9   ♣ Q 6 5 2

(v) ♠ 9 7   ♡ A J 9 7   ♦ K 2   ♣ K J 8 4 3

(w) ♠ 9 7   ♡ A J 9 7   ♦ J 5   ♣ J 9 5 4 3

With (t), bid an obvious, forcing 2♡.

Hand (u) is too weak for 2♡, tempting though it is. Double is best. If partner rebids 2♣, pass while over 2♦, continue with 2♡, non-forcing.

Whenever reasonably possible, bid naturally. With (v), bid 2♣, just as you would without the overcall. Over the likely 2♦ rebid, continue with 2♡, natural and forcing. Similarly, continue with 3♡ after a 2NT rebid.

It is inferior with start with a negative double just to show the heart holding. If partner rebids 2♦, you cannot afford to rebid 3♣, as that would not be forcing. You could continue with 2♠ to force to game, but that is not nearly as descriptive as the natural auction.

Hand (w) is too weak for a forcing 2♣ response. That leaves double as the best action, much better than passing. The double promises hearts and 6+ points and allows you to pass if partner rebids 1NT, 2♣ or 2♦.

Bidding the Enemy Suit

Once again partner opens 1♦ and next player overcalls 1♠. What would you do with these hands?

(x) ♠ 9 8 2   ♡ K J 8 3   ♦ A 7 5   ♣ A Q 4

(y) ♠ 9 8 2   ♡ K J 8   ♦ A 7 5   ♣ A Q 4 2

With (x) double first, showing 4+ hearts, and if that fails to uncover a 4-4 heart fit, continue with 2♠, hoping that partner can bid no-trumps.

With (y), bid 2♠ at once, asking for a spade stopper and denying four hearts (failure to double first).

Chapter 5

The Takeout Double

If partner makes a takeout double, consider it as a three-suited overcall. Partner has a hand of about opening values, tends to be short in their suit and is asking you to suggest the denomination.

The primary focus in making a takeout double with minimum values is any unbid major. If right-hand opponent (RHO) opens 1♡, what do you do with these hands?

(a) ♠ A Q 7 3   ♡ 9   ◇ K 7 4   ♣ Q 8 4 3 2

(b) ♠ K 7 4 3   ♡ - - - ◇ A Q 7 3 ♣ 9 8 4 3 2

(c) ♠ A Q 7 3   ♡ 9 4   ◇ K 8 3   ♣ A J 4 2

(d) ♠ A Q 7 3   ♡ 9 4   ◇ A Q   ♣ K 8 4 3 2

(e) ♠ K Q 5   ♡ 9   ◇ A Q 4 2 ♣ K 9 7 3 2

(f) ♠ K 9 7 3 2 ♡ 9   ◇ A Q 4 2 ♣ K Q 5

Hand (a) is a typical minimum takeout double. It is borderline, but your spades are good and partner will give priority to bidding spades. (Reverse the spades and diamonds and you should pass.) Whether partner bids 1♠, 2♣ or 2◇ you will accept that and pass.

With a three-suiter and a void in their suit, you need little to make a takeout double. Double with (b), which is a suitable minimum.

Hand (c) has less promising shape but is clearly worth a takeout double. In the minimum doubling zone, below 16 HCP, your shortest suit needs to be the enemy suit.

Hand (d) is even less attractive, because of the diamond shortage, but it is still worth a double. You will be happy to hear a reply in spades, no-trumps or clubs and will pass 2◇, likely to be a five-card suit as partner bypassed so many bids on the way to 2◇.

With (e) and (f), the choice is between a double and an overcall. The importance of the major suit is reflected in the approach chosen.

With (e) a takeout double is best. The hand is too strong for a pass and a 2♣ overcall suggests a stronger suit and not a three-suited hand.

With (f), the fifth spade tilts the scale in favour of a 1♠ overcall despite the suit quality. The advantage of the overcall is that partner will expect a 5+ suit and can support with three trumps. The overcall also leaves you better placed if the auction becomes competitive, for example:

(g)	South	West	North	East	(h)	South	West	North	East
		1♡	1♠	2♡	No		1♡	Dble	2♡	No
	No	?				No	?		

After (g), West can continue comfortably with a takeout double. Partner will read West to hold five spades and tolerance for each minor.

After (h), West has an awkward choice. 2♠ is not an option, as that sequence shows a far stronger hand than this. West can make a second takeout double, but a 5-3 spade fit could be lost.

Strong Hands

What would you do with these hands after RHO opens 1◇?

(i) ♠ A Q J 8 4   ♡ A J 7   ◇ 8 3   ♣ A K J

(j) ♠ A Q J 8 4 3   ♡ A 7   ◇ 8 3   ♣ A J 7

(k) ♠ A Q J 8 4 3   ♡ A 7   ◇ A 3   ♣ A J 7

(l) ♠ A Q   ♡ A J 7   ◇ A J 10 8 ♣ A 10 9 4

With all of these, too strong for a simple overcall, you should start with a takeout double. When you double for takeout and bid again after a minimum reply, you are showing a strong hand.

With (i) and (j), double and bid spades at the cheapest level after a 1♡ or 2♣ reply. That will show a hand too strong for a 1♠ overcall. It does not imply a two-suited hand.

Hand (k) is stronger still and warrants a double followed by a jump in spades. With (l) double and then bid no-trumps at the cheapest level, showing 19-21 HCP, too strong for a 1NT overcall.

Because the takeout double is essentially forcing, it allows you another call after partner replies to the double. This allows you to double with a strong hand but a shape without tolerance for all unbid suits.

Suppose RHO opens 1♦. What would you do with these hands?

(m)   ♠ A Q J 7 3   ♥ A Q 4 2   ♦ 9 4   ♣ 9 6

(n)   ♠ A Q J 7 3   ♥ A Q 4 2   ♦ 9 4   ♣ K 6

(o)   ♠ A Q 7 3   ♥ A J 9   ♦ 9 4   ♣ A K Q 2

With (m), the best option is 1♠. This hand is not strong enough to double and remove a 2♣ response to 2♠.

Hand (n) with five losers is one trick stronger and you can start with a double. If partner responds in a major, you will be delighted. If partner responds 2♣, you deduce that there is no fit in hearts and continue with 2♠. This shows a 5+ suit and a strong hand. Partner can expect 16 HCP or more and usually a five-loser hand.

With hand (o), you start with a double and, not surprisingly, partner replies 1♥. What next? Having only three-card support argues against a heart raise and the recommended approach is to bid the enemy suit, 2♦ here. This shows a powerful hand and is forcing for one round. If partner can do no more than 2♥, you should pass. With a hand which warrants game opposite around a 20-count, partner needs to do more than 2♥ by bidding either no-trumps or a new suit.

Suppose partner's reply to your takeout double is a pleasant surprise. With support for partner, how high should you raise? Consider the following hands after the auction has started this way:

South	West	North	East
1♥	Double	No	1♠
No	?		

(p)   ♠ K 9 7 3   ♥ 9   ♦ A Q 6 4   ♣ K 9 8 3

(q)   ♠ K 9 7 3   ♥ 9   ♦ A Q 6 4   ♣ A Q J 3

(r)   ♠ A Q 7 3   ♥ 9   ♦ A Q 6 4   ♣ A Q J 3

A certain degree of caution and conservatism is required. Your double forced partner to bid and a minimum suit reply can contain no high cards and no ruffing values. On a really bad day partner might have been obliged to bid a three-card suit. A sound approach is to imagine that you opened the bidding with a minor suit and partner responded at the one-level, here 1♠. Decide to what level you would have raised and then support partner to one level less than that.

With (p) you would raise a 1♠ response to an opening bid to 2♠ and so in this context, you should pass.

With (q), you would raised a 1♠ response to 3♠ and so a 2♠ rebid is appropriate for the doubler. Likewise, with (r) you should bid 3♠ here, as you would raise a 1♠ response to an opening bid to 4♠.

Suppose the bidding had been:

South	West	North	East
1♡	Double	No	1♠
2◇ / 2♡	?		

What action would you now take with hands (p), (q) and (r)?

It is almost always right to do the same thing you would have done if opener had passed. Thus with (p) you should pass to confirm a minimum double. East is still there to compete with suitable values. Similarly, with (q) you still bid 2♠ and with (r) 3♠.

Now consider this auction:

South	West	North	East
1♡	Double	2♡	2♠
No	?		

Now you should feel confident that partner has some values. As North's bid has freed East of the obligation to bid, East has made an unforced bid of 2♠ and so will not have just three spades. The failure of South to bid higher also suggests that East has a respectable hand. What sort of a hand might East have? Normal expectation is around 6-9 points but less is possible with a good suit and a high ODR.

	South	West	North	East
	1♡	Double	2♡	?

(s) ♠ Q J 10 9 2   ♡ 8 7 3 2   ◇ 9 3   ♣ 6 4

(t) ♠ 9 5 4 3   ♡ Q 8 3 2   ◇ J 8 2   ♣ Q 6

With hand (s) East should bid 2♠ despite the low point count. The strong suit, the fifth trump and the high ODR justify that. With (t), a borderline case, it is better to pass. The suit is poor and the ODR is significantly higher than in (s).

The doubler therefore treats East's 2♠ as equivalent to a minimum 1♠ response to an opening bid. The doubler should pass with this:

(p)   ♠ K 9 7 3   ♡ 9   ◇ A Q 6 4   ♣ K 9 8 3

What about with these?

(q)   ♠ K 9 7 3   ♡ 9   ◇ A Q 6 4   ♣ A Q J 3

(r)   ♠ A Q 7 3   ♡ 9   ◇ A Q 6 4   ♣ A Q J 3

With (q) one might not criticise 3♠ but the value bid is 4♠. Put hand (s) opposite hand (q) and you have a strong chance to make 4♠ with a combined total of only 19 HCP. Remember that finesses taken through the opening bidder are likely to succeed.

With (r), bid 3♡ first and follow up with 4♠. This suggests slam, and 6♠ is highly likely to succeed opposite as little as—

♠ K 9 8 6 2   ♡ 7 5 3 2   ◇ K 8   ♣ 6 4

Responding to a Takeout Double

You are expected to reply to partner's takeout double no matter how miserable your hand. Weakness is no excuse for passing. To pass a takeout double at the one- or two-level is very rare. It should be a positive action based on a desire to play in their suit as trumps, not a shrug of helplessness because you have nothing worth saying.

South	West	North	East
1♦	Double	No	?

What would you do as North with these hands?

(u) ♠ 8 4 3   ♡ 10 5 2   ♦ J 8 4 3   ♣ 9 6 3

(v) ♠ 9 8   ♡ A 7   ♦ K Q J 9 8 6   ♣ 9 6 3

(w) ♠ J 7 3 2   ♡ J 8 3 2   ♦ 9 5 4   ♣ 6 4

(x) ♠ Q J 7 3   ♡ K 10 7 4   ♦ 9 5 4   ♣ 6 4

(y) ♠ A J 7 3   ♡ K J 10 4   ♦ 9 5 4   ♣ 6 4

With (u) grit your teeth and bid 1♡. This is why the doubler must exercise some caution when raising partner's suit.

With (v), you should pass. The penalty pass is rare and requires better trumps than declarer is likely to have. The doubler is expected to lead a trump if possible so that declarer's trumps can be drawn.

Hands (w) and (x) have the same shape but your strategy depends on the hand strength and whether you are worth a second bid if the auction develops along either of these lines:

South	West	North	East	South	West	North	East
1♦	Dble	No	1♡/1♠	1♦	Dble	No	1♡/1♠
No	No	2♦	?	2♦	No	No	?

With (w) you are not worth another bid unless partner forces you to bid again and therefore you may as well bid 1♡, the cheaper suit. That allows West to introduce spades cheaply if hearts do not appeal.

With (x) you are strong enough to show both majors and so should bid 1♠ first. Then when you compete with 2♡, partner can pass or give cheap preference to 2♠.

Hand (y) also has both majors and is worth a cue-bid of 2♦. This action used to be forcing to game. Nowadays it is forcing to suit agreement (a suit bid and supported). Your plan is to raise partner's 2♡ or 2♠ rebid to the three-level to invite game.

South	West	North	East
1♦	Double	No	?

What would you do as East with these hands?

(a) ♠ J 9 5 3   ♡ 8 4   ♦ 6 2   ♣ J 9 7 5 4

(b) ♠ Q J 5 3   ♡ 8 4   ♦ 6 2   ♣ K 10 9 4 3

(c) ♠ Q 8 4 3   ♡ 7 4   ♦ Q 9 5 4   ♣ 9 4 3

(d) ♠ Q 8 4 3   ♡ 7 4   ♦ A 9 5 4   ♣ 9 4 3

(e) ♠ 8 5 3 2   ♡ 8 4   ♦ K Q 10 8   ♣ Q 4 3

(f) ♠ A Q 9 5 3   ♡ 8 6 4   ♦ 9 8 4 2   ♣ 9

(g) ♠ J 7 3 2   ♡ 8 4   ♦ A K 9   ♣ J 8 4 3

In general it is best to show the major suit first, even with a longer minor. The order of priorities is majors first – no-trumps second – minor suits last. To bid a minor suit is generally taken as denying a major. Thus with (a) and (b), bid 1♠. With (b) there is a temptation to bid 2♣ first in the hope of being able to bid spades next time. The danger is that there may be no next time.

With (c), (d) and (e) the question is whether to bid 1♠ or 1NT. Hand (c) is too weak for 1NT, which shows about 6-9 points, akin to a 1NT response to an opening bid. Hand (d) is more offensive for spades and so 1♠ is an easy choice. With (e), a 1♠ bid is also reasonable but with the poor spades and powerful diamond holding, we would opt for a 1NT bid, despite the usual recommendation. If facing a singleton, ♦K-Q-10-8 is likely to be more useful in no-trumps than in spades.

High card points are not the only criterion in deciding whether you are too strong for a suit bid at the cheapest level. With (f) you are well worth a jump to 2♠. The strong suit, the fifth trump and the singleton all give you a high ODR and justify the jump reply.

Hand (g) has the values for 2♠ and that would be our choice. Still, it is close between 1♠, 2♠ and 1NT and if you chose 1NT because of the lack of quality of the spades, that is no heinous crime.

Other takeout doubles

South	West	North	East	
1♥	No	2♥	Double	East's double, takeout of hearts, shows the other three suits.

South	West	North	East	
1◇	No	1♥	Double	The double shows the unbid suits, clubs and spades here.

East should have opening strength or better. With fewer points and at least a 5-5 pattern in the unbid suits, a conventional 2NT jump would be available (see Chapter 7).

South	West	North	East	
1NT	No	2♣	Double	Assuming 2♣ is Stayman, the double shows long, strong clubs.

It is a general principle that a double of a conventional bid shows the suit doubled and asks partner to lead that suit if partner is on lead.

South	West	North	East	
1NT	No	2♥	Double	The meaning of double depends on the meaning of 2♥.

If 2♥ is a weakness sign-off and shows hearts, then the double is for takeout. If 2♥ is a transfer to spades then the double shows good hearts and you can bid 2♠, the enemy suit, for takeout.

South	West	North	East	
1♥	No	1NT	Double	The double of a 1NT response is for takeout of the suit opened.

This is an exception to the rule that the double of a no-trump bid is for penalties. As the auction indicates that opener and responder have virtually half the points in the pack between them, you would wait a long time before you were strong enough to be confident of defeating 1NT. Even then they may retreat to a suit contract. It is far more efficient to treat this double as a takeout of hearts, the suit opened.

South	West	North	East	
1◇	No	1♥	No	West's double is a takeout of hearts. Shortage in hearts explains why you passed first time.
2♥	Double			

Chapter 6

Opener's Partner Bids after a Double

An overcall after your partner's opening bid usually takes away your bidding space. A takeout double cuts out none of your bidding space, indeed it gives you another option, the redouble. Before considering how other bids are affected by the double it is important to be clear how the redouble is used.

The Redouble

South	West	North	East
1♥	Double	?	

Redouble by North would show at least 10 HCP and expresses an interest in doubling whatever contract East-West might reach.

(a)   ♠ K J 10 8   ♡ 8   ◇ A Q 10 4   ♣ Q 10 9 8

(b)   ♠ K J 10 8   ♡ 8 5   ◇ A K 10 8   ♣ 8 5 2

(c)   ♠ K J 10 8   ♡ 8 5 2 ◇ A K 10 8   ♣ 8 5

(d)   ♠ K 9 5 4   ♡ 8 5 2 ◇ A 9 7   ♣ A 10 2

(e) ♠ 9 8   ♡ 8 5   ◇ A 7 4   ♣ A Q J 7 4 3

Hand (a) is perfect for a redouble. North is eager to double any East-West contract. Not only does North have excellent intermediate cards (tens and nines) but the shortage in South's heart suit is an excellent omen for defensive prospects. The same singleton that signifies a misfit for offence increases the prospect of South making heart tricks without running into a ruff. Hand (a) has a very low ODR opposite a partner whose main suit is hearts.

Hand (b) is also suitable for a redouble. This time North will be delighted to double a spade or diamond contract. With such poor trumps, North will not double a club contract, but will be happy if South can double it.

Hand (c) is slightly less suitable for a redouble, mainly because North has three hearts. The ODR is a little higher than would be ideal, but still redouble is the best available option. If East bids 2♣, passed back to North, best is to continue with 2♥. As the redouble denied a fit for opener's suit, 2♥ will indicate mere tolerance.

With hand (d) North cannot feel much enthusiasm for doubling anything, but it is still best to start with redouble. Unless South doubles an enemy contract North's next action is likely to be 2NT to show a balanced 11-12 count. Given West's double it is not attractive to introduce a paltry spade suit.

How about hand (e)? In the early days of Acol it was common to double on any hand without 4-card support for partner, provided that you had ten or more points. Consequently change-of-suit by responder was limited in strength and therefore not forcing. The problem with this approach can be seen if the auction develops as follows:

South	West	North	East
1♥	Double	Redouble	1♠
No	3♠	?	

As you have advertised strength with the redouble, the opponents are eager to push the bidding as high as they dare. You cannot introduce your excellent club suit below the four level. Nowadays if North has a single-suited hand with 10+ points, it is best to bid it. Here North bids a natural and forcing 2♣.

Be very wary of introducing a bad suit after a takeout double. Suppose South opens 1♥, West doubles and you hold:

♠ J 8 4 3   ♥ 9 8   ◇ K 8 3 2   ♣ Q 6 4

You should pass. Without the double you would have been obliged to introduce your scraggy 4-card spade suit, but there is little to be gained from this now. Even if you find a 4-4 spade fit you might regret it, as it is quite likely to be one of West's suits. Replace the ♣Q with the ♣A and a 1NT response, 7-10 points, would be sensible.

South	West	North	East
1♡	Double	Redouble	?

If North had passed East would be duty bound to bid unless East had the rare hand that is suitable for a penalty pass. According to one school of thought, East takes the same action as though North had passed, including the penalty pass option. The more popular view is that a pass by East simply means that East has nothing to say, not that East is itching to defend 1♡ redoubled.

(f)	♠ J 8 5 4	♡ 9 7 4 3	◇ 8 3 2	♣ 9 4
(g)	♠ 9 4	♡ 9 7 4	◇ J 10 8 6 5	♣ 9 7 2
(h)	♠ 8 3 2	♡ 9 7 3 2	◇ J 8 5 4	♣ 9 4
(i)	♠ 8 3	♡ K Q J 10 6 5	◇ J 8 5	♣ 9 4
(j)	♠ Q J 10 8 4	♡ 9 7 4 2	◇ 9	♣ J 9 8

With (f) East bids 1♠. It might be unpleasant to play in 1♠ doubled, particularly if it happens to be a 4-3 fit, but if East passes West might bid a minor suit with even worse consequences.

With (g) East bids 2◇. This raises the level of the contract, but East does strongly prefer diamonds to anything else.

With (h), the first school of thought bids 1♠ so as not to advertise the weakness of the hand and the absence of direction. The popular style is for East to pass and let West suggest a strain. If West rebids 1♠ at least the contract is at the one-level. For East to bid 2◇ ahead of West could well be a similarly unpleasant trump fit one level higher.

With (i) the first school of thought passes for penalties. For the majority, East would love to defend 1♡ redoubled, but it cannot happen! If East passes West will play East for a hand like (h) and remove to 1♠, or even worse, 2♣. East must anticipate this by bidding 1NT. If this is doubled East will then retreat to 2♡, and it will take a very dim West to misunderstand East's intentions.

After a redouble, jump-bids do not show strength but are pre-emptive. With a fit, put the opponents under maximum pressure. With (j) jump to 2♠. West's heart shortage and East's diamond shortage suggest that in a spade contract a lucrative cross-ruff will develop.

How should opener react? North's redouble has created a forcing situation. Both partners are aware that East-West cannot be allowed to play in a contract undoubled (except in the rare case when they have a fit and are voluntarily bidding higher rather than scrambling to avoid trouble). The sort of auctions which make it clear that East-West are not afraid of being doubled are below. In each case North-South should feel free to pass out 2♠ if there is no suitable alternative.

South	West	North	East		South	West	North	East
1♡	Dble	Rdble	No		1♡	Dble	Rdble	1♠
No	1♠	No	2♠		No	2♠	No	No
No	No	?			?			

Suppose the bidding has been:

South	West	North	East
1♡	Double	Redouble	No
?			

What should South do with these hands? What would your answer be if East had bid 1♠?

(k) ♠ 9 6   ♡ A J 10 7 3   ◇ K 8 3   ♣ A J 7

(l) ♠ K J 10 4   ♡ A J 8 3 2   ◇ 10 8   ♣ A 7

(m) ♠ 8   ♡ A Q 10 8 4 3   ◇ 9   ♣ Q J 9 8 4

(n) ♠ 8   ♡ A Q 10 8 4 3   ◇ 9   ♣ A K J 9 8

It is normal for opener to pass unless able to double for penalties or with extreme distribution. With (k), South passes in both cases. With (l), South passes unless East bids 1♠, which South doubles for penalties. In both cases, with (m), bid 2♣ to show a sub-minimum opening, low in defence and high in distribution, and with (n), bid 3♣, forcing to game, to show a powerful, highly distributional hand.

South	West	North	East
1♡	Double	Redouble	1♠
No	No	Double	No
?			

What should South do with these hands?

(o)   ♠ 8   ♡ A Q 8 4 3   ◇ 9 6 2   ♣ K Q J 4

(p)   ♠ - - - ♡ A Q 10 8 4 3   ◇ 9 6 2   ♣ K Q J 4

Once partner doubles for penalties, it is normal for opener to pass, and that is what South would do with (o). With a void in their suit, it is unwise to play for penalties at a low level and so with (p), South removes the double to 2♣. This shows a respectable opening since South would have bid 2♣ on the previous round with a sub-minimum, shapely hand.

The redoubler promises another bid and if a penalty double is not appropriate, some other bid must be chosen.

South	West	North	East
1♡	Double	Redouble	1♠
No	No	2♡ . . .	

North is showing a minimum redouble with three-card support. The position is non-forcing. Likewise 2NT by North would be natural, showing a balanced 11-12 points, not forcing. 3NT would be natural with 13+ points.

South	West	North	East
1♡	Double	Redouble	1♠
No	No	2◇ . . .	

A new suit by the redoubler is forcing, analogous to any change of suit response to an opening suit bid. North's 2◇ creates an auction equivalent to 1♡ : (No) : 2◇ . . .

With enough for game but no obviously natural bid to describe the hand, North can bid the enemy suit, 2♠ here, to force to game.

One of the consequences of using the redouble on balanced hands (rebidding 2NT with 11-12 and 3NT with 13+) is that there is no need for a natural 2NT to show a balanced hand of 11-12 points. A more useful purpose for 2NT in this context is to show a hand of redoubling strength (10+ HCP) with 4+ support for opener's suit. Thus, redouble denies support, 2NT guarantees support.

	South 1♡	West Double	North ?	East
(q)	♠ 9 4	♡ K 8 4 3	◇ 8 4 3	♣ 9 4 3 2
(r)	♠ 9 4	♡ K 8 4 3	◇ 8 4 3	♣ A 4 3 2
(s)	♠ 9 4	♡ K 8 4 3	◇ 8 4 3	♣ A K 3 2
(t)	♠ 9 4	♡ K 8 4 3	◇ K 4 3	♣ A K 3 2
(u)	♠ 9 4	♡ K J 6	◇ A 7 4 3	♣ 10 7 4 3

With 4-card support for opener, a sensible approach after a double is to raise one level higher than you would have raised without the double.

With (q) bid 2♡. With (r) bid 3♡, showing a 4-card raise to 2♡.

With (s) jump to 2NT. This is forcing as far as 3♡. If not interested in game, opener signs off in 3♡. With hand (s), you would pass 3♡.

With (t) you again start with 2NT, but this time if opener signs off in 3♡ you raise to 4♡. This shows a balanced raise to 4♡, as distinguished from a direct raise to 4♡, which suggests a shapely hand but less high card strength, just like a 1♡ : (No) : 4♡ raise.

That leaves hand (u). You would bid 2♡ without the double, but what should you do now?

Regrettably there is no better bid than 2♡ available now. Inevitably this makes it hard for opener to judge what to do if a raise to 2♡ can be made on (q) and on (u) as well. Because of this some now play the jump to 3♡ as purely pre-emptive, as with hand (q), and 2♡ as constructive, as on hands (r) and (u).

Chapter 7

Two-suited Overcalls

A takeout double followed by a change of suit does not at that point show a two-suited hand. It may be a one-suiter too strong for a simple overcall. However it is important to be able to show two-suited hands with at least a 5-5 pattern, particularly because two-suiters tend to have a high ODR. In addition if partner is short in one of your suits, there is a good chance that partner will have support for the other suit.

Whatever conventional gadget you use to show a two-suiter it is important to discuss the strength expected. Suppose you play that over a 1 ♦ opening a 2 ♦ overcall shows the majors. How can partner judge what to do if your 2 ♦ bid can be made on any of these hands?

(a) ♠ K Q 10 9 5   ♡ Q J 9 8 5   ♦ 5   ♣ 8 4

(b) ♠ A Q 10 9 5   ♡ A K 10 7 5   ♦ 5   ♣ 8 4

(c) ♠ A K J 10 7   ♡ A K J 9 5   ♦ 5   ♣ 8 4

The popular solution is to classify them according to strength:

Weak is 6-10 high card points, such as hand (a).

Intermediate is 11-15 high card points, such as hand (b).

Strong is 16+ high card points, such as hand (c).

Use your two-suited overcall only on the weak or strong types. Partner will assume you have the weak type and if this is correct you will pass partner's choice of contract. If you do have the strong type you will bid on. It is worth noting the potential of (a) and (c).

Hand (a) has a high ODR with almost no defence against a diamond contract. Perhaps each side can make a high level contract and so it is very much in your interest to stake a claim. Be wary of competing at red vulnerability, but being able to show both suits in one bid gives you an excellent prospect of finding a major suit fit, so do not be put off.

Hand (c) has only 16 HCP, but give partner as little as ♠Q-3-2 and you would be prepared to try for game. The hand is very powerful in offence, but you cannot be certain that 5♦ can be defeated.

Once 2♦ is not available, you would overcall 1♠ with hand (b). Hopefully you will be able to compete in hearts later, for example:

South	West	North	East
1♦	1♠	3♦	No
No	3♥ . . .		

Partner will realise that you have a hand of intermediate strength and act accordingly.

Suppose RHO opens 1♦. What would you do with:

   ♠ Q 7 6 4 3   ♡ J 8 5 4 3   ♦ K   ♣ A 9

With 7 of your 10 points in your short suits and few tens and nines in your long suits, this hand has a low ODR. Therefore pass. Not every 5-5 pattern qualifies for a two-suited overcall. Reject the hands where the long suits have poor quality.

Once you decide that you want to play two-suited overcalls, what bids are available? An easy candidate is the cue-bid of an opponent's suit. To play it as a game-forcing hand, as was the custom, is a very inefficient use of this cue-bid. Such a hand is rare after an opponent's opening bid, and in any case if you have a very powerful hand that needs input from partner you can easily start with a takeout double and then cue-bid the enemy suit on the next round.

A jump to 2NT is also available to show a two-suiter. With a very strong, balanced hand you start with a double and then bid no-trumps. A jump-overcall in a new suit is not available if playing it as natural but there is a case for a conventional use for a jump to 3♣.

That gives you two (or perhaps three) bids at your disposal. There are two basic types of two-suited overcalling systems you can use. One (Ghestem) shows the two suits held but needs the jump to 3♣ to do so. The other (Michaels) leaves the second suit unspecified in some auctions and that can be costly in a competitive auction.

Suppose, at game all, the bidding has started:

South	West	North	East
1♠	2♠	4♠	?

2♠ showed hearts and a minor suit. What should East do with:

♠ 8 5 4 2   ♡ Q 8   ♢ K 8 7 5 4 2   ♣ 9

Had North passed, East could have easily discovered West's second suit but East has an unwelcome dilemma now. If West has the red suits East should definitely bid on. It is quite possible in that case for 4♠ to make North-South and 5♢ East-West. Thus if East knew West had the red suits, it would be automatic for East to bid 5♢.

In practice, with the minor suit unknown, East would pass since it is far more likely that West has hearts and clubs. By competing further East could be walking into a minefield of minus 1400 proportions or worse. Since it natural for East to assume that West has hearts and clubs, it is possible that a wonderful diamond fit will never see the light of day.

Two approaches follow and you are left to choose the system with which you feel most at home.

Ghestem

There are several versions of Ghestem. As there is little to choose between them, only one is given here.

After an opposition opening bid of 1 ♢, 1 ♡ or 1 ♠:

2NT shows the two lowest-ranking unbid suits.
3♣ shows the two highest-ranking unbid suits.
A cue-bid shows the extreme suits.

Therefore, over a 1♢ opening, 2NT = hearts and clubs, 3♣ = the majors and 2♢ = clubs and spades.

After an opposition opening bid of 1 ♣:

2♢ shows diamonds and spades.
2NT shows the red suits.
3♣ shows the majors.

You are free to change the order in which the two suits are shown but a word of warning. To avoid conflict with the opponents and the Tournament Director, if you play Ghestem make sure your convention card is filled in accurately and that you know your system.

Michaels Cue-Bid and the Unusual No-Trump

While Ghestem has the advantage of pinpointing the suits held, the Michaels Cue-Bid and the Unusual No-Trump are more widely played.

The Michaels Cue-Bid involves an immediate bid of opener's suit. If the opening bid is a minor suit then the cue-bid shows the majors, weak or strong. If their opening bid is a major, the cue-bid show the other major and one of the minors. Thus:

(1♣) : 2♣ = hearts and spades

(1♢) : 2♢ = hearts and spades

(1♡) : 2♡ = spades plus either clubs or diamonds

(1♠) : 2♠ = hearts plus either clubs or diamonds

Playing Michaels, you are East and faced with this auction:

South	West	North	East
1♣	2♣	No	?

What action would you take with these hands:

(d) ♠ Q 8 4   ♡ K 7 4   ♢ 9 7 5 4   ♣ J 3 2

(e) ♠ K 8 4 3 2   ♡ Q 4 3   ♢ 9 4 2   ♣ 6 4

(f) ♠ K 8   ♡ J 6 3 2   ♢ A 9 4 2   ♣ A K 6

Always assume partner has the weak option. With (d) bid 2♡. If minimum, West will pass. Suppose West continues with 2♠. West is now known to be strong, and has longer spades than hearts, presumably 6-5 shape. (With equal length in the majors and strong, West would have bid 3♡.) With two useful honour cards in the major suits you should now jump to game in 4♠.

South	West	North	East
1♣	2♣	No	?

(e) ♠ K 8 4 3 2   ♡ Q 4 3   ◇ 9 4 2   ♣ 6 4

With (e) East should pre-empt to 4♠. If West has a weak hand South must be very strong and East should seek to silence South. If West is strong then 4♠ will make in comfort. Note that West should not look for a slam here even though holding the strong variety. A jump to 4♠ (or 3♠) shows a weak, distributional hand. With a strong hand, East would not jump in a major but instead start with a cue-bid of 3♣.

(f) ♠ K 8   ♡ J 6 3 2   ◇ A 9 4 2   ♣ A K 6

West has already cue-bid their suit and with (f) East makes a further cue-bid of 3♣ to show the powerful hand. West, who almost certainly has the weak type, will bid a major and East then continues with 4♡.

When the opposition's opening bid is a major suit then the Michaels Cue-Bid shows the other major suit and a minor, again weak or strong. What should you do with hands (g) and (i) after this start:

South	West	North	East
1♡	2♡	No	?

(g) ♠ 8 4 3   ♡ K 7 3   ◇ Q J 8 4   ♣ A 8 2

(h) ♠ 8   ♡ 9 4 3   ◇ K 8 4 3   ♣ J 8 4 3 2

(i) ♠ K 8 5   ♡ A 6 3   ◇ A Q 4 2   ♣ 9 7 4

With (g) East has no cause for enthusiasm and bids a peaceful 2♠.

With (h) bid 2NT, asking West to show the second suit. With the weak option West bids 3♣ or 3◇ and you will pass in either case. If strong, West will jump to 4♣ or 4◇ and you will raise to game.

With (i), you also bid 2NT. If partner bids 3◇, jump to 4♠ because of the double fit. If partner bids 3♣, bid 3♠, inviting game. Without game interest you would have bid 2♠ over 2♡, as with (g).

As mentioned earlier the fact that you do not know partner's minor suit after a Michael's Cue-Bid can make life difficult if RHO jumps to game. Nevertheless when you know that a trump fit must exist, you can still locate the right suit. Suppose the auction begins:

South	West	North	East
1♡	2♡	4♡	?

What would you do with these hands at equal vulnerability?

(j)　♠ 8 4 3 2　　♡ 9 7 3　　◇ A J 8 4　　♣ 8 2

(k)　♠ 8　　　　♡ 9　　　◇ K 8 6 4 2　♣ 9 7 6 5 3 2

With (j) bid 4♠ as a sacrifice. You cannot expect to defeat 4♡ and given West's shape, the cost of 4♠ doubled figures to be less than their 4♡ making. If you are lucky, they may push on to 5♡.

With (k) East wants to compete in West's minor suit, sacrificing if West is weak or expecting to make if West is strong. Had North passed, East would have bid 2NT to ask for the minor suit. Now East bids 4NT to ask for West's minor. This cannot be natural because with enough to try 4NT opposite West's weak type, East would be doubling 4♡. It is an example of the unusual 4NT for takeout. Plenty of other examples will appear later in this book.

South	West	North	East
1♡	2♡	4♡	No
No	?		

What should West do with these hands?

(l)　♠ K Q 8 4 3　♡ 7 3　　◇ A J 10 8 7　♣ 9

(m)　♠ A Q J 9 3　♡ 7　　◇ A K 10 8 3　♣ A 4

With (l), you pass. You have said it all with 2♡.

With (m) you double. This is neither a takeout double, nor a penalty double. It simply shows the strong type. East can pass if that seems best, otherwise East can bid 4♠ or ask for the minor with 4NT.

In competitive auctions 4NT is often used to seek the best trump fit. The idea gained acceptance after the jump-overcall to 2NT had become the norm as a takeout at the two-level.

After an opponent opens with one-of-a-suit, a 2NT overcall shows the two lowest unbid suits, either weak or strong. Over a major, it shows both minors, while over a minor it shows hearts and the other minor. It is called the Unusual No-Trump and in each case the overcaller's two suits are known. The advancer, overcaller's partner, uses the same principles in responding as after a Michaels Cue-Bid.

When playing Ghestem all two-suiter combinations are covered. This is not so for the Michaels Cue-Bid and Unusual No-Trump structure where there is no two-suited overcall to show spades and the other minor if an opponent opens with a minor suit. With this holding, your options are to overcall one spade and hope to be able to bid the minor later if partner cannot support spades or, if the hand is very strong, start with a double.

Extreme Distributions

Suppose South opens 1 ♡. What should West do with these?

(n) ♠ K Q J 9 8 3   ♡ - - -   ◇ A Q 10 9 8 7   ♣ 9

(o) ♠ K Q J 9 3   ♡ - - -   ◇ A K J 8 4 3 2   ♣ 8

Forget about points when you have such mighty playing strength (only three losers) and a huge ODR. If you decide to use a two-suited overcall, 2H, you naturally treat them as the strong type.

Hand (n) is highly suitable for 2♡, but suppose the auction develops as follows :

South	West	North	East
1♡	2♡	4♡	No
No	?		

What would you do now?

A double would indeed show the strong type, but that is not a wise move. East would have every reason to place West with more points but less dramatic distribution and might well pass for penalties, leading to a less than optimum outcome. West should continue with 4♠ over 4♡. If East dislikes spades East can always continue with 4NT, asking West to show the minor suit.

Hand (o) is indeed a two-suiter, but not remotely suitable for 2♡. It often works out badly to make a two-suited overcall when you have a difference of two cards or more in the length of your suits. It is easy to imagine playing in 4♠ (perhaps doubled) with partner having a low doubleton in each of your suits. You may then be forced to shorten your trump holding by ruffing hearts and the hand could fall apart as your opponents wrest trump control from you.

The answer with hand (o) may surprise you. Bid 2♢. Yes, just a simple 2♢! Admittedly your playing strength is far greater than partner can envisage but this is merely the beginning. Do not fret that 2♢ might be followed by three passes. That will not happen even once in a blue moon. You have only 14 high card points, leaving quite a few for your partner and opponents. As you have extreme shape it is quite likely that the others also have shapely hands. Somebody will bid again and you can then complete the description of your hand by leaping to 4♠. This now shows five spades and hence longer diamonds, as they were bid first. Note that an immediate 3♢ would be ill-judged, because that would increase the danger that your bid will be passed out. You want to encourage competition!

Likewise, another option for hand (n) is to start with just a 1♠ bid. If partner can support spades, you will keep on with the spades and may make a high-level contract doubled, as you have given the opposition no inkling of your extreme shape. If partner does not support spades, you can bid diamonds on the next round, 5♢ if they have bid 4♡.

Incidentally, there are players who abuse the Unusual No-Trump by making the bid with a 6-4 pattern. This could lead to your playing in a 4-3 fit with a far superior 6-2 fit gone begging. You cannot expect partner to make a successful choice if you provide such poor data.

Overcalling Their 1NT Opening Bid

There is a crucial difference between a two-suited overcall after their suit opening and a similar action after they open 1NT. Most strong hands start with a double of 1NT, making it unlikely that you would start with a two-suited bid. Your overcall after their 1NT will therefore tend to be intermediate (up to 15 points), or weak. Stronger, unbalanced hands will be considered later.

Whether you insist on at least a 5-5 pattern, or whether you permit a 5-4 shape depends on personal taste and perhaps whether you are playing teams-of-four or duplicate pairs. At pairs it is often imperative to dislodge your opponents from a 1NT contract, even at considerable risk, but for the time being assume that you are playing teams-of-four. In that case a two-suited overcall should show good ODR and partner should look for game with a suitable hand and useful values. The most popular style is to allow the overcaller to bid with 5-4 shape.

There are plenty of conventions in this area, some of which specify both suits and others which show one suit (the 'anchor' suit) and an undisclosed second suit. The pros and cons are very similar to the arguments outlined earlier. These are two common approaches:

The Landy Defence to 1NT

In this simple conventional defence to 1NT, 2♣ shows both majors (at least 5-4 shape). The other two-level suit overcalls are natural.

The Astro Defence to 1NT

Double = Penalties (all strong hands except those with extreme shape).
2♣ = hearts and a minor suit, with at least 5-4 shape.
2♦ = spades and a minor suit, with at least 5-4 shape.
2♥ or 2♠ shows a single-suited hand.

Advancing after the 2♣ overcall:
2♦ is a non-forcing inquiry for the cheapest 5-card suit. With five diamonds the 2♣ bidder passes.
2♥ is a sign-off (maybe with only 3 hearts); 3♥ is invitational.
2♠, 3♣ or 3♦ is natural and forcing.

The 2NT advance after 2♣ is conventional and forcing, asking for the second suit. Advancer might be intending to pass the rebid, or advancer might be strong and looking for the best game contract.

Advancing after a 2◇ overcall follows the same principles, with 2♡ being the non-forcing inquiry for the 5-card suit and 2NT the inquiry bid for a strong hand.

Overcalling their 1NT with 2NT

With most strong hands you start by doubling 1NT with the intention of scoring penalties. With a strong two-suiter and a high ODR, it is better to introduce a game-forcing two-suiter with 2NT. Take a look at these hands:

WEST	EAST	West	North	East	South
♠ K Q J 7 4 3	♠ 6 5 2				1NT
♡ A 8	♡ J 9 4 3 2	2NT	No	3♣	No
◇ A K J 10 7	◇ 6 3	3◇	No	3♡	No
♣ - - -	♣ 9 6 4	3♠	No	4♠	All pass

After 2NT, East starts with the cheapest suit for which East has tolerance, 3♣ shows at least three clubs, 3◇ shows one of West's suits, 3♡ shows heart tolerance and West now shows the other suit. East supports spades as 4♠ is the most likely game contract.

There are two reasons why it would not pay West to start with a double. Firstly, if you double, North may remove to some number of clubs. You are unlikely to beat a low-level club contract and after you cue-bid in clubs and reach 4♠, the auction may influence the opponents to sacrifice in clubs.

Secondly, if North does pass 1NT doubled you may well find yourself unable to beat it. On the above hand South has at least six tricks: five club tricks and the ♠A. Give North six or more clubs and 1NT doubled will be unbeatable. Even if you do manage to take 1NT one off, that would be a very poor return when you can make 4♠.

Chapter 8

1NT in Competition

Doubling Their 1NT Opening Bid

Suppose RHO opens 1NT, 12-14. What would you do with these:

(a) ♠ K J 8   ♥ Q 9 7 6   ♦ K Q 4   ♣ A J 6

(b) ♠ 9 3   ♥ A 7 2   ♦ K Q J 10 8 6   ♣ A 6

(c) ♠ 9 3   ♥ 8 4   ♦ A K Q J 10 4 3   ♣ 8 5

If you have a balanced hand, the recommended minimum to double an enemy weak 1NT opening bid is 16 points. Hand (a) is suitable.

You might reasonably decide to double with fewer points if you have a strong suit and a good lead, such as hand (b). It is tempting to double with hand (c). After all you are on lead and you can certainly beat 1NT but there are two good reasons not to double.

Firstly, you have no defence to any contract other than no-trumps. You will have no idea what to do if opener's partner jumps, say, to 4♠ and partner doubles! Partner will undoubtedly be expecting far more defensive values than you possess.

Secondly, if you pass it is not impossible that responder may raise no-trumps and you could find yourself on lead against 3NT. With (c) it is best to pass. If they remain in no-trumps you will be pleased to take your tricks. If they remove to a suit contract you are likely to have an opportunity to bid your diamonds at a reasonably cheap level, particularly if they are playing transfers, for example:

South	West	North	East
1NT	No	2♥	No
2♠	3♦ ...		

What are North's priorities if South opens 1NT and West doubles? It is normal to abandon Stayman and transfers, because the priority is to escape from what might be a considerable mess. You undoubtedly need to be able to sign off at the two-level in any of the four suits. For the time being we will look at natural bids by North, although you might prefer the 'wriggle' that appears later in this chapter.

South	West	North	East
1NT	Double	?	

What should North do with these hands?

(d) ♠ Q 8 5 4 2   ♡ K 10 4   ◇ 7 3   ♣ K Q 2

(e) ♠ 9 7 3   ♡ 8 4 3   ◇ A 3   ♣ 9 7 4 3 2

(f) ♠ 6 5   ♡ 8 4   ◇ A K J 6 4 3   ♣ 9 7 4

North should bale out in 2♠ with hand (d). It is a mistake to argue that since North-South have the majority of high card points 1NT doubled will make. With kings and queens rather than aces, North has slow tricks, tricks that need time to be developed. If West holds a hand like (b) opposite, South will not have time to develop tricks.

With a weak hand and any five-card or longer suit, it will usually be safer to play in the suit contract than to stay in 1NT doubled. With hand (e), North should run to 2♣, a natural bid asking opener to pass. This does not come with guarantees. Opener might have a doubleton club but the North hand is likely to take more tricks if clubs are trumps than the probable sole trick with the ◇A in no-trumps.

Hand (f) gives North a difficult decision. The safe course of action is to sign off in 2◇. However, with a buccaneering spirit North may choose to pass. On a lucky day 1NT doubled will make, probably with overtricks. On a less lucky day 1NT doubled can be two or three off. The point is that although (f) is weaker than (d) in HCP, it will be possible to take your tricks more quickly than with (d). If South needs the diamond finesse in 1NT doubled, it will be through the hand that doubled 1NT and so it is likely to succeed.

The next player to face a decision is the doubler's partner.

South	West	North	East
1NT	Double	No	?

What action East take with these hands?

(g) ♠ 7 6 4 2   ♡ 8 5 3   ◊ 7 5 2   ♣ 9 3 2

(h) ♠ 7 4   ♡ 8 5 3   ◊ 7 5 2   ♣ J 10 9 4 3

(i) ♠ 7 4   ♡ K Q J 10 8 5 3   ◊ 7 5   ♣ 9 2

The old notion that East should always run with a weak hand is unsound. To run to any suit contract here might lead to a four-figure penalty. There are two good reasons for East to pass. If West has a hand such as (b) on page 58, 1NT doubled will be defeated without any help by East. Secondly, if 1NT doubled makes with a couple of overtricks, that will be minus 380 not vulnerable and minus 580 if they are vulnerable. This figures to be much cheaper than the penalty you are likely to incur in such a scenario if you run to 2♠. Even if North redoubled for business East should pass and allow West to take out the double into some contract possibly cheaper than 2♠.

To decide whether or not to remove your partner's double of 1NT because you are very weak, you must consider each hand on its merits. Vulnerability is clearly a factor and the following guide-lines will help.

Firstly, rarely, if ever, remove 1NT doubled into a 4-card suit.

Secondly, you should be more inclined to remove 1NT into a low-ranking suit. Disaster is unlikely if you remove 1NT doubled to 2♣ with (h). If partner has an unbalanced hand and hates clubs, partner can easily bid another suit cheaply at the two-level.

You do not automatically leave 1NT doubled in because you are strong. With (i) you should not pass. In no-trumps your hearts may not come into play until too late. Even if partner leads hearts, not very likely, declarer may be able nullify their value by a simple hold-up play. You will usually do much better by jumping to 4♡.

How should doubler's partner act if responder bids a suit?

South	West	North	East
1NT	Double	2♡	?

What should East do with these hands?

(j) ♠ 9 4   ♡ Q J 9 8   ◇ A 7 4 2   ♣ 9 7 4

(k) ♠ K J 7 3   ♡ 8 3   ◇ A J 9 2   ♣ 9 7 4

(l) ♠ K 7   ♡ A Q   ◇ Q 9 4 3 2   ♣ 9 7 4 2

(m) ♠ K J 7 3   ♡ 8 3   ◇ 9 4 3 2   ♣ 9 7 4

The first priority is to decide on the meaning of double by East. A sound idea is to follow the practical, wide-ranging and easy-to-remember principle that once one partner has made a penalty double, or has turned a takeout double into a penalty double by passing, then all subsequent doubles are for penalties. Thus East should double with (j). This shows a strong trump holding and that the doubling side holds the majority of points.

With (k), cue-bid 3♡, forcing to game but suggesting that East cannot tell the right denomination. If West bids 3♠, East will happily raise to 4♠, while if West bids 3NT, East will pass.

With (l), it is worth taking a shot at 3NT. You have the values for game and the hearts well stopped. The lack of length in hearts makes it unlikely that a penalty double will be sufficiently profitable.

That leaves something of a problem with (m). You want to compete but naturally there is an uneasy feeling that 2♠ should show a five-card suit. Some pairs play a pass here as forcing West to bid again. This would be convenient with this hand, but could be fatal if East had nothing and West had a balanced 16 points. A sound approach is that pass by East means, 'I have nothing to contribute'. If you adopt this, then East can improvise with 2♠ with (m). The points are likely to be roughly 20-20 between the two sides and East-West may have a 4-4 spade fit. The LTT says that it is right to compete if they have a trump fit and so somebody has to take the initiative in bidding a 4-card suit.

If you play the weak no-trump you do have to accept stoically the occasional unpleasant penalty. However, if you play a 'wriggle' you can increase your chances of escaping unscathed.

South	West	North	East
1NT	Double	?	

Try the following 'wriggle' if you are in the North seat:

1. Redouble requires opener to bid 2♣ (a puppet manoeuvre). When opener duly bids 2♣, responder may pass with club length or bid another suit, which will be at least five cards long.

2. 2♣, 2♦ or 2♥ shows the suit bid and a higher-ranking suit.

What action would you take as North in the above auction with these hands if you have agreed to play the 'wriggle'?

(n) ♠ K J 7 3   ♥ Q 7 4 3   ♦ 9 4   ♣ 8 3 2

(o) ♠ Q 8 5 4 3   ♥ 9 4 3   ♦ 9 4   ♣ 8 3 2

(p) ♠ J 8 4 3 2   ♥ 9 4   ♦ Q 8 7 5 3   ♣ 9

(q) ♠ Q J 6 3   ♥ 9 4 3   ♦ 9 4   ♣ J 9 4 3

With (n) North bids 2♥. This shows both majors as North bids the cheaper suit held.

With (o) North redoubles and then converts 2♣ to 2♠, a sign-off.

With (p) North bids 2♦. Opener is expected to pass this with three or more diamonds. If opener bids 2♥, North will rebid 2♠.

With (q) North bids 2♣, which shows clubs and another suit. Again South is expected to pass with three-card or better support. Sometimes such a wriggle succeeds in uncovering a 4-4 fit. The rest of the time you find at worst a 4-3 fit. If South bids 2♦, North rebids 2♠.

West	North	East	South
1NT	Double	?	

As the redouble is used with a 5+ suit in a one-suited hand and the cheaper suit is bid with a two-suiter, what would 2♠ or 2NT by East mean? You may have your own ideas but one possibility is to use these bids for hands with game prospects and a high ODR, at least a 5-5 pattern. Thus, 2♠ could be 5+ spades and a long other suit in an invitational hand, while 2NT can be used for an invitational 5-5 without spades or any game-force two-suiter.

WEST	EAST	West	North	East	South
♠ A 7 4 3	♠ K Q 9 5 2	1NT	Dble	2♠	No
♡ A K	♡ 8	4♠	No	No	No
◇ J 9 7	◇ Q 8 6 5 4 2				
♣ 8 7 5 2	♣ 4				

If East passes 1NT doubled, this is likely to fail by at least one trick. If East runs to 2◇, bidding the cheaper suit, West will pass and an excellent 4♠ contract will be missed. A penalty double of your 1NT opening does not eliminate the possibility of game for your side, especially when responder has a highly distributional hand.

Lebensohl

Partner opens 1NT and the next hand overcalls with a natural 2♡. Your planned response may now be unavailable. You have lost 2♣ as a Stayman inquiry to investigate a 4-4 spade fit. You may wish to compete in a minor suit or force to game with an unbalanced hand. In addition, it would be prudent for at least one partner to have a stopper in hearts if you aim to be in 3NT. The popular Lebensohl convention is very effective in solving these problems.

Top priority is given here to finding the best contract when game is available. To do this you must be prepared to give up a natural 2NT response. Instead 2NT is used as a puppet to 3♣. That means that if responder bids 2NT over the 2♡ overcall, the 1NT opener is compelled to bid 3♣. A puppet bid does not show anything specific but forces partner to make the cheapest possible bid.

In the Lebensohl convention, if the 1NT opening bid is overcalled with a natural 2♡, responder bids as follows:

(1) Double is for takeout, with game invitational values.

(2) 2♠, a new suit at the two-level, is competitive, not invitational.

(3) 2NT requires opener to bid 3♣. It can be used for a number of different purposes:

  (i) Responder can pass 3♣, using the puppet to compete in clubs.

  (ii) Responder can continue with 3♢ to compete in diamonds.

  (iii) Responder can continue with a cue-bid of 3♡. This shows game values with a 4-card major (obviously spades), but no heart stopper.

  (iv) Responder can continue with 3NT. This denies a 4-card major and also denies a heart stopper.

(4) A new suit at the three-level is natural and forcing to game.

(5) 3♡ (a cue-bid) shows a heart stopper and four spades.

(6) 3NT shows a heart stopper but denies four spades.

If all this seems hard to memorise then there are a couple of *aide-memoires*. All game-forcing hands without a heart stopper start with the 2NT relay. All hands with a 4-card major use the cue-bid of 3♡. Remember: *2NT = no stopper; bidding their suit = 4-card major*

(Some pairs use 2NT when a stopper is held and the immediate cue-bid and 3NT as stopper-denying. It does not matter which way you go as long as both partners are on the same wavelength.)

WEST	EAST	West	North	East	South
♠ K Q 9 2	♠ A J 8	1NT	2♡	2NT	No
♡ 9 5 4	♡ 8 6 2	3♣	No	3NT	No
♢ A 8	♢ K 7 6 3	4♣	No	4♢	No
♣ K J 6 2	♣ A Q 5	4♠	No	No	No

2NT followed by 3NT denies a heart stopper or a 4-card spade suit. West realises that 3NT will probably fail and so tries 4♣. 4♢ and 4♠ show 4-card suits, and East realises that they are unlikely to improve on the 4-3 fit. 4♠ is almost certain to succeed while 3NT is very risky.

How does Lebensohl work when your opponents overcall with an artificial bid? The basic structure of Lebensohl bidding is the same as if the overcall was natural. The difference is that you may have to worry about two suits, one of which you know and one which you do not know. Worry about the one you know, for the very practical reason that you cannot do anything about the second suit.

Suppose that partner's 1NT opening is overcalled with 2♢ (Astro), showing spades and another suit. Responder bids as follows:

(1) Double of an artificial bid shows that suit, i.e., diamonds. Opener is invited to compete with a diamond fit.

(2) 2♡, a new suit at the two-level, is competitive.

(3) 2♠, their anchor suit, is for takeout, showing at least game invitational values.

(4) 2NT requires opener to bid 3♣.

(i)   Responder can pass 3♣, using the puppet as a competitive move.

(ii) Responder can continue with a new suit (3♢ or 3♡) showing the values to invite game and a 5-card suit.

(iii) Responder can continue with a cue-bid of 3♠. This shows the values for game with a 4-card major (obviously hearts), but without a spade stopper.

(iv) Responder can continue with 3NT. This denies 4 hearts and also denies a spade stopper.

(5) 3♠ (a cue bid) shows a spade stopper and four hearts.

(6) 3NT shows a spade stopper but denies 4 hearts.

WEST	EAST	West	North	East	South
♠ 10 8 3	♠ 7 2	1NT	2♢	2NT	No
♡ A Q 8 2	♡ K J 10 4	3♣	No	3♠	No
♢ A K 6 2	♢ Q J 7 3	4♡	No	No	No
♣ 9 5	♣ A K 2				

2♢ = Astro, spades and another suit. East's 2NT-then-3♠ showed the values for game, with 4 hearts but no spade stopper.

A 1NT opening bid is often played as showing 12-14 points. There are two reasons why it would be foolish to play a 1NT overcall as showing 12-14, too. Firstly, the average 12-14 point hand with a stopper in their suit does not have a high enough ODR to make interference necessary or attractive.

Secondly, a 1NT overcall is far more likely to be doubled than a 1NT opening bid. Whenever opener's partner has 10 points it is easy to double in the knowledge that their side has the majority of points. Unlike a penalty double of a suit contract, which requires good trumps as well as high cards, the side with a clear majority of points can usually dictate the play in a no-trump contract. If 1NT is doubled, often there are few entries to dummy to take vital finesses, so declarer is continually endplayed into leading broken suits from hand.

A 1NT overcall is generally played as 15-18 high card points and at least one stopper in their suit. A double stopper would be preferable but you cannot afford to wait for that before overcalling 1NT. To overcall on 15 points you should have good features in your hand to compensate, for example, more than your fair share of nines and tens, or a 5-card suit that might be a source of tricks. This would be a suitable minimum 1NT overcall of 1♡.

♠ K 7   ♡ A J 10   ◇ K Q J 8 5   ♣ J 10 5

With a running suit, you can fudge a few points. You can bid 1NT over 1♡ with this collection.

♠ 10 4 3   ♡ A 7   ◇ A K Q 10 4 3   ♣ 10 7

Ideally a 1NT overcall should show a balanced hand, but life is not always that simple. Suppose RHO opens 1♡. What do you do with:

♠ 9   ♡ A J 10 4   ◇ K Q J 10   ♣ A K 7 3

1NT is far from ideal but it is the least flawed action. Passing could easily result in missing a game and to double with shortage in spades is asking for trouble.

If partner overcalls 1NT, use the same conventional structure as you would opposite a 1NT opening bid, except that you require fewer high card points to justify a move towards game. You should certainly use Stayman and transfers, and there is no good reason why you should not use Lebensohl and a wriggle if responder competes.

What do you make of the East-West sequence in this auction?

West	North	East	South
1♡	1NT	2◇	2NT
No	3♣	No	3◇
No	3NT	All pass	

2NT is the Lebensohl puppet to 3♣. The cue-bid of 3◇ shows a game-going hand with a four-card major (clearly spades) and no diamond stopper. East need not worry about a stopper in hearts, the other enemy suit, because West's 1NT already promises a heart stopper. West bids 3NT to indicate that there is no 4-4 spade fit.

You might be surprised that East-West have game values when South can open the bidding and North can introduce a new suit at the two-level, but North needs few values for 2◇, as will be seen shortly.

	South	West	North	East
	1♡	1NT	?	
(r)	♠ 9 8 2	♡ 7 5	◇ K J 10 9 4 3	♣ 8 7
(s)	♠ 9 5 2	♡ K 9 5 3	◇ 10 9 4 2	♣ 6 3
(t)	♠ 9 5 2	♡ K 10 9 4 3	◇ K 10 4 2	♣ 7
(u)	♠ K Q J 7 4 3	♡ 7	◇ K J 10 4 3 2	♣ - - -
(v)	♠ K J 8 3	♡ 9 5	◇ A Q 6 3	♣ 8 3 2

With (r), bid 2◇, not forcing. A forcing 2◇ is unnecessary because if strong you double. 2◇ shows a good suit, usually with 6+ cards.

With (s), bid 2♡. Even though West has a heart stopper, 4♡ might make if South is strong and distributional. With (t), jump to 3♡.

South	West	North	East
1♡	1NT	?	

(u) ♠ K Q J 7 4 3   ♡ 7   ◇ K J 10 4 3 2   ♣ - - -

With (u), you want to investigate game prospects, especially if vulnerable against non-vulnerable opponents. Start a forcing auction by bidding 2NT. This is analogous to the 2NT overcall after their 1NT opening. It cannot be natural because with a balanced 10-12 points you would double for penalties.

(v) ♠ K J 8 3   ♡ 9 5   ◇ A Q 6 3   ♣ 8 3 2

With (v), double for penalties. You know that your side has the majority of the high card points so 1NT is unlikely to make. Any subsequent double should be for penalties, again following the principle that once one partner has made a penalty double then all subsequent doubles are for penalties.

It makes sense to treat this penalty double as an agreement that North-South should not be allowed to play in any contract undoubled. Suppose the auction continues:

South	West	North	East
1♡	1NT	Dble	2♣
No	No	?	

South's pass of 2♣ does not necessarily show a minimum opening. This is an example of a forcing pass. South does not have clubs strong enough to double 2♣ for penalties but is giving North the chance to double. Once you have the chance to collect penalties, you do not want to let them off the hook if possible.

Hand (v) is not suitable for doubling clubs but in view of the above agreement after a penalty double, North must not pass. The best move at this point is to bid 2◇.

Chapter 9

Protective Bidding

The Transferred King

So far it has been stressed that when considering intervention over RHO's opening bid you should carefully consider your ODR and, if in doubt, ask whether the lead directing consequence of the overcall is likely to be helpful. The upshot is that you would pass a $1\heartsuit$ opening on your right with these cards:

♠ 10 7 5 4 3   ♡ 9 6   ♢ K J 6   ♣ A K J

However if responder also passes $1\heartsuit$, your partner cannot afford to be as choosy, otherwise it is all too possible that $1\heartsuit$ is passed out when your side has game-going values. A few undoubled undertricks will hardly be adequate compensation.

South	West	North	East
$1\heartsuit$	No	No	?

Even if game is not available for your side, there are other reasons for being more competitive in the pass-out seat. Consider East's action with the hand above if South's $1\heartsuit$ opening is followed by two passes. It is likely that North-South have at least seven hearts between them. Remember that advice from Chapter 2, namely, *Try not to let your opponents play at a level equal to their number of trumps.*

There is every chance that North-South have at least seven hearts and as $1\heartsuit$ is likely to make, it is important to compete for the part-score. East should therefore bid 1♠.

Here are some more useful guides:

Do not sell out to their suit at the one- or two-level if short in their suit.

A suit overcall in the pass-out seat does not promise any suit quality.

And also from Chapter 2, *Try to bid to the level equal to the number of trumps held by your side.*

South	West	North	East
1♡	No	No	?

East and West have different considerations. West can pass in the knowledge that East still has an opportunity to speak. East's position is final. If East passes then South has won the auction. The immediate overcaller, West, is said to be in the 'direct seat', while the player in the pass-out seat, East, is in the 'protective' or 'balancing' position. The 'rule of the transferred king' is an excellent guideline for balancing. *Mentally add a useful king to the cards held.* Here, for example:

♠ 10 7 5 4 3   ♡ 9 6   ◇ K J 6   ♣ A K J

East may replace the ♠3 with the ♠K. If the resultant hand with that extra king would have been worth a bid in the direct seat, then East makes that bid in the protective seat. Would West have bid over 1♡ with:

♠ K 10 7 5 4   ♡ 9 6   ◇ K J 6   ♣ A K J

Since the answer is an emphatic 'yes', East should protect with 1♠.

After the above auction, what should East do with these hands:

(a)   ♠ A J 10 6 5   ♡ 9 5 4   ◇ J 9 8   ♣ 8 6

(b)   ♠ J 9 5 4 3   ♡ A K 8   ◇ Q 3 2   ♣ 9 7

(c)   ♠ 8 5   ♡ K 8 4   ◇ 7 5   ♣ A J 9 6 5 3

(d)   ♠ A K 10 7 5 ♡ A 6   ◇ K 8 3   ♣ 10 9 7

(e)   ♠ K Q 4 3   ♡ 9 8   ◇ A 9 6 5 4   ♣ K 9

(f)   ♠ A Q J 8 5 4 ♡ 8 5   ◇ A J 9   ♣ 8 6

(g)   ♠ K J 8 3   ♡ 9   ◇ A 8 7 3   ♣ J 7 4 3

(h)   ♠ 8 7   ♡ A J 10 4 3 ◇ A 8 6 ♣ A 4 3

Hand (a) is an example of a minimum protective one-level overcall. Note that there is little danger in bidding 1♠. South could open with only 1♡ and North could not even summon up a reply. East knows that West must have quite a few points. Of course West must realise that East is bidding some of West's points, a king's worth, and not respond too enthusiastically.

Hand (b) is also worth 1♠, despite the feebleness of the spade suit. Experience indicates that the likely destination of this hand is 2♠ played by East, or perhaps North-South will compete further at the three-level to their detriment. One thing is certain, the LTT makes it clear that to sell out to 1♡ is a losing strategy.

Hand (c) is an example of a minimum two-level protective overcall.

Hand (d) is too strong for a protective 1♠. East should double, and then bid spades at a minimum level.

Similarly hand (e) should start with a double. To bid 2♢ runs too great a risk of missing a spade fit. If partner bids 2♣, continue with 2♢.

With hand (f) East should jump to 2♠ at any vulnerability. It is sensible and common practice to play intermediate jump-overcalls in the protective seat, whatever your preferences in other positions.

Hand (g) is an example of a minimum protective takeout double. Add a useful king to your hand and the action becomes straightforward.

With hand (h), you have the option of passing or balancing with 1NT. While a direct 1NT overcall is 15-18 points, the protective 1NT need not be so strong. The advantage of bidding is that you may reach a successful contract. The advantage of passing is that you are very strong in South's suit and have good chances to beat 1♡. By bidding you may enable South to find a better trump fit, which you may be unable to defeat. The strong clue is West's silence. If West is short in hearts, West will not be strong, else West would have doubled. If West is not short in hearts, South will have a torrid time in 1♡. While the decision is not clear-cut, you will be usually do better by passing borderline hands which are long and strong in the enemy suit.

South	West	North	East
1♢	No	No	?

What should East do with these hands?

(i)   ♠ J 8 4   ♡ 8 7 4 3   ◇ A J 9   ♣ A Q 8

(j)   ♠ Q 8 4   ♡ K J 3   ◇ 9 8 3 2   ♣ A K J

(k)   ♠ J 10 4   ♡ A J 5   ◇ A Q 8 6   ♣ A J 7

(l)   ♠ K Q 4   ♡ A J 5   ◇ A Q 8 6   ♣ A J 7

With hand (i) East should bid 1NT. A 1NT protective overcall is best played as wide-ranging, 11-16 points. With game interest West can continue with 2♣ to clarify the range and the major suit holdings. The 1NT overcaller's replies to the 2♣ inquiry are:

2◇ = 11-12 HCP, any balanced pattern. If this is not enough for game, West can now show a 4-card major with 2♡ or 2♠ or bid 2NT with no major. If still interested in game, West can jump to 3NT with no major or bid 3◇, the enemy suit, to ask for a 4-card major.

2♡ or 2♠ = 13-14 HCP with four cards in the suit bid. Over 2♡, 2♠ or 2NT would not be forcing. Likewise over 2♠, 2NT is not forcing. With enough for game, West can bid it or bid 3◇.

2NT = 13-14 HCP with no 4-card major.

Any three-level bid shows 15-16 HCP which has to be enough for game if partner has shown game-interest. The three-level bids here are natural except for 3◇ which denies a sound stopper in diamonds.

With hand (j) you could double but with length in their suit it is better to bid 1NT even though you have no stopper in their suit. If you are left in 1NT, you can afford to lose up to six tricks and if West bids on in no-trumps, West is likely to have a stopper. If concerned about the diamond position, West can always bid diamonds with or without using the 2♣ inquiry.

Hand (k) is too strong for a protective 1NT. Start with a double, with the option of bidding no-trumps next time.

Finally, with hand (l) East jumps to 2NT, which shows a balanced hand with 20-22 HCP, the same as a 2NT opening. Note that even if you play the unusual no-trump, it is normal to abandon it in the protective position. Firstly, because a protective 1NT overcall has such a weak lower limit you are short of bids to show a strong balanced hand. Secondly, since the bidding was about to die at the one-level there is no need for an unusual 2NT to suggest a sacrifice.

Although you are urged to protect, there are times when it can be risky. Suppose the bidding has been 1♣, pass, pass, to you. What would you do with these hands?

(m) ♠ 9 8   ♡ 8 3   ◇ K Q J 10 9 7   ♣ Q J 3

(n) ♠ 9 8   ♡ 7 3   ◇ K J 10 8 5   ♣ A Q 10 7

No doubt you feel that it would be an act of craven surrender to pass with (m), but how will you feel if you protect with 1◇ and North-South proceed to bid 4♡ or 4♠? You have little defence against either of these contracts and, given West's silence, it is highly likely that North-South have an 8-card fit in at least one of these suits. Best is to pass, but if you must bid, at least make life difficult for your opponents by pre-empting to 3◇.

With (n) the danger is even greater. If West is short in clubs then West must have a poor hand to pass 1♣. Alternatively if West has some length in clubs then North-South are in a poor contract and should be left to their fate. Given West's pass, chances for game for your side are remote. Hand (n) illustrates the danger of protecting when you have too much in the enemy suit.

The Protector's Partner

Perhaps the advice of this section is a statement of the obvious, but it still needs emphasising. If East adds a king before deciding what to bid, then West must subtract a king in response, otherwise there will be severe overbidding. Thus, in reply to a protecting suit bid, deduct three points from your hand and then make the appropriate bid.

South	West	North	East
1◇	No	No	Double
No	?		

What should West do with these hands?

(o) ♠ 9 8 4   ♡ A 6 2   ◇ K Q 7 3   ♣ Q 8 3

(p) ♠ A Q 10 8   ♡ K 9   ◇ J 8 4 3   ♣ 9 8 3

(q) ♠ A 8   ♡ K 9 2   ◇ Q 10 8 3 2   ♣ K 8 5

With (o), bid 1NT, which in this situation shows 9-12 HCP rather than the usual 6-9. Would you want to be any higher than 1NT if East has a minimum protective takeout double?

With (p), you would bid 2♠ opposite a direct seat double but facing a balancing double, 1♠ is quite sufficient.

With (q) take a chance and pass. Of course you would not pass a direct seat takeout double of 1◇ with such a moth-eaten diamond suit, but here your diamonds are sitting over declarer's and dummy figures to be very weak. If East has 10+ points and one or two diamonds, defending 1◇ doubled should be quite lucrative. If they run from 1◇ doubled perhaps East can deal with that.

Other Protective Situations

South	West	North	East
1♡	No	2♡	No
No	?		

In this auction North-South have found a fit, yet they are content to make no move towards game. Two things should strike you. Firstly, the fact that they have found a fit greatly increases the prospect that your side has a fit. Secondly, the greater their fit, the more likely they are to investigate game, so on this auction you can expect the points to be divided roughly evenly between the two sides. You should look for any excuse to enter such an auction regardless of the vulnerability.

After the foregoing auction, what should West do with these hands?

(r) ♠ K 8 5 4 3   ♥ 9 7   ♦ A 7 3   ♣ 10 7 2

(s) ♠ A Q 10 8   ♥ 9 8 7   ♦ K 7 4   ♣ 10 9 7

(t) ♠ K J 8 3   ♥ 9 8   ♦ J 8 7   ♣ A 6 4 3

(u) ♠ A Q 5   ♥ 8 5 4   ♦ K J 9   ♣ A 9 8 2

(v) ♠ A 7   ♥ K Q J 9 7   ♦ K 8 4   ♣ 9 8 4

With (r) protect with 2♠. With (s), although it would be no crime to pass, a 2♠ overcall will work more often than not.

With (t) protect with a takeout double. Likewise with (u) a takeout double is preferable to a cowardly pass.

With (v) you have to pass. It would be delightful to double for penalties but since double is for takeout that option does not exist. You will rarely hold such a hand after North and South have found a fit.

South	West	North	East
1♥	No	1♠	No
2♦	No	No	?

What would you do after this start if you hold:

♠ A 6 3 2   ♥ K 8   ♦ 9 7   ♣ K Q 9 7 6

The time to be wary is when opponents have no certain fit. 3♣ would be very dangerous. Consider the evidence. Firstly, North's failure to give preference to 2♥ suggests that West has length in hearts. Secondly, South's second suit may only have four cards and North's failure to raise may mean that North does not have four diamonds.

Thirdly, although it is possible that your side has half of the points in the pack, it is also possible that South has 17-18 points (not quite strong enough for a jump-shift). In that case a bid of 3♣ by you could find your opponents catching up and bidding game, or doubling you for a blood-bath.

In some auctions there can be a very wide range of hands for partner in the balancing seat.

South	West	North	East
1NT	No	2♡	No
No	?		

West might double for takeout with either of these hands:

(w)   ♠ K J 8 3   ♡ 9   ◇ A Q 8 7   ♣ A J 9 8

(x)   ♠ K J 8 3   ♡ 9   ◇ Q 8 7 2   ♣ J 10 9 5

With (w) West was nearly strong enough to double 1NT. Hand (x) is much weaker but West can afford to double as East is marked with reasonable strength. What should East do with these cards if West has doubled after the above beginning?

♠ A 7 4 2   ♡ 8 4 3 2   ◇ K J   ♣ Q 6 3

Opposite (w) 4♠ is an excellent contract. On the other hand if West has (x) then 2♠ is quite high enough. The golden rule in these situations is to give partner some leeway. If you go looking for game on the off-chance that partner has the perfect hand then the resulting minus scores will make partner reluctant to compete with modest values. That will lead to many part-scores conceded to the opponents when you might have scored a part-score your way or pushed them beyond their safety level. It is worth mentioning that partner will more often have the weaker hand type and you do not want to stifle partner's competitive urge.

In competitive situations, do not punish your partner for showing enterprise. If you do, partner will gradually become ultra cautious.

Of course after protective action both sides must be vigilant to preserve their interests. In deciding how far to compete the LTT, together with your ODR, should be your guiding light.

South	West	North	East
1♡	No	2♡	No
No	2♠	No	No
3♡			

Which of these hands justify the above 3♡ bid by South?

(y)   ♠ 9 3   ♡ A Q J 8   ◇ K 9 4 3   ♣ A J 7

(z)   ♠ K Q 10   ♡ A 7 4 3 2   ◇ A 8 4   ♣ Q 4

(a)   ♠ 9 3   ♡ K Q J 8 6   ◇ A Q 10 4   ♣ 9 4

In general South should have a fifth heart for this bid, otherwise there is the danger that South is competing to the three-level with only seven total trumps. Possession of the fifth heart is far more important than the point count. North could have bid 3♡ without suggesting extra strength and the failure to do so carries an inference of holding only three-card support.

With (y) South should pass. South's card are excellent for defence and the ODR is low.

With (z) South should pass, too. Admittedly South has that vital fifth heart, but in every other respect South has a low ODR. With four hearts and a reasonably high ODR North could have competed to 3♡, and so there is some indication that North has either only three hearts or a poor ODR also.

Hand (a) is the weakest of the three hands, but it is the most suitable for 3♡. With a fifth heart and a high ODR, South should seek to buy the contract in 3♡, or push East-West to 3♠.

South	West	North	East
1NT	No	No	2♡
No	No	?	

What should North do with these cards after the above auction?

   ♠ J 10 7 4   ♡ 8 3   ◇ K 9 5   ♣ A 10 7 6

South	West	North	East
1NT	No	No	2♡
No	No	?	

♠ J 10 7 4   ♡ 8 3   ◇ K 9 5   ♣ A 10 7 6

Do not sell out to 2♡. East-West have at least seven hearts between them and quite probably eight. Best is a takeout double. Occasionally South will have excellent hearts and can pass for penalties. Otherwise South will remove the double, with 2♠ as first priority.

Note that even if you prefer to play double for penalties after an opponent overcalls partner's 1NT, double here should be for takeout. The crucial point is that any heart holding you have is sitting under East's suit and so finesses will work for East. You are more likely to catch opponents for a worthwhile penalty by playing double for takeout and allowing partner to profit on those occasions when the hearts are stacked over the 2♡ bidder.

Pre-balancing

So far we have assumed that protective action only applies when the hand is about to be passed out. However consider this situation:

WEST	EAST	Dealer South : Any vulnerability			
♠ J 8 4 2	♠ K Q 5 3	West	North	East	South
♡ 9 4 3 2	♡ 6				1NT
◇ A Q 3	◇ K 8 4 2	No	2♡*	?	
♣ A 5	♣ 10 8 6 4	*Natural, sign-off, not a transfer			

As North-South can make 2♡ and East-West 2♠, who should take the responsibility of entering the auction? West has more points than East, but East (the hand with short hearts) has a much easier decision to compete with a double. If East passes, so will West.

East knows that North-South have limited their hands and do not intend to bid higher than 2♡ voluntarily. Thus East is as much a protective hand as West. This is called 'pre-balancing'. Again West must not punish East for enterprise. 2♠ in response to East's double is quite high enough!

Chapter 10

More Takeout Doubles

The Responsive Double

The most lucrative doubles of a low-level contract occur when an opponent has entered the auction, perhaps with an overcall, only to find partner with a misfit and the missing trumps breaking unkindly. After a suit has been bid and raised, a fit clearly exists and the opponents do not fear being doubled. Therefore, it would be inefficient to use the double by South in these auctions for penalties.

West	North	East	South	West	North	East	South
1♡	Dble	2♡	Dble	1♣	Dble	3♣	Dble

A sensible alternative is to play South's double for takeout. The message is that South wants to compete but wants North to choose the denomination. South's double in this context is known as a 'responsive double'. This is a double by the partner of the takeout doubler after responder raises opener's suit. South is considered to be responding to the takeout double with another takeout double.

If the opposition suit is a minor suit, the responsive double shows equal length in the major suits. To be doubling 3♣ in the second auction above, South might hold something like:

♠ K J 7 3   ♡ K Q 10 6   ◇ 9 7 2   ♣ 10 8

Had East raised to just 2♣, South could have a weaker hand.

If the raised opposition suit is a major, then the responsive double denies 4+ cards in the other major and asks partner to choose a minor. South's double of 2♡ in the first auction might be based on this:

♠ J 2   ♡ 8 5 3   ◇ K J 8 5   ♣ K 10 8 7

The rationale behind the proliferation of low-level takeout doubles is that if opponents have found a fit at a low level it is seldom in your best interests to make a penalty double. What should South's double mean in this auction:

West	North	East	South
1♡	1♠	3♡	Double . . .

It would be perfectly plausible to play the double for takeout, based on holding both minor suits. However, a more efficient use exists.

Had East raised to just 2♡ South could have bid 2♠ or 3♠ competitively or made a game try in spades with an unassuming cue bid of 3♡. After the jump to 3♡, South can have two conflicting aims, to compete in spades for the part-score and to invite game in spades. A bid of 3♠ cannot fulfil both functions.

(a)   ♠ K 9 3 2   ♡ 8   ◇ K J 4 3 2   ♣ 9 5 4

(b)   ♠ K 9 3   ♡ 8   ◇ K J 4 3 2   ♣ A 9 5 4

With (a) South wants to compete with 3♠ (LTT) but has no serious ambitions for game. With (b), game is possible opposite a maximum overcall. One solution is to bid a competitive 3♠ with (a) and use Double as a game try with (b). Hence the name, *Game Try Double*.

The situation is similar in this auction:

West	North	East	South
1♡	2◇	2♡	3◇
?			

West may wish to compete to 3♡ or to invite game. The 3♡ bid cannot be the servant of two masters. The approach adopted by most top players to cater for such dilemmas is to bid the agreed suit (3♡) merely to compete and to double as a game invitation. Clearly this is an area that needs close partnership understanding, including whether the double is also a game try if North had passed.

To bid $3\heartsuit$ in the preceding auction, West should have at least five hearts and a high ODR and not enough strength to warrant a game invitation. This would be a suitable candidate:

$\spadesuit$ A 8 4 $\heartsuit$ K Q 10 9 7 6 $\diamondsuit$ 9 2 $\clubsuit$ K 8

To use the game try double in the same sequence, West would have a hand that would invite game after the single raise with or without the opposition intervention. This would do:

$\spadesuit$ A Q 4 $\heartsuit$ K Q J 8 6 $\diamondsuit$ 9 2 $\clubsuit$ A J 9

The Competitive Double

West	North	East	South	West	North	East	South
$1\heartsuit$	$1\spadesuit$	$2\heartsuit$	Dble	$1\heartsuit$	$1\spadesuit$	$2\clubsuit$	Dble

What do you make of South's double in each of these auctions?

As penalty doubles of low-level suit contracts are unattractive when opponents have bid and raised a suit, the double of $2\heartsuit$ is more useful for takeout. It is not needed as a game try in spades because the $3\heartsuit$ is available for that purpose. Such doubles for takeout are known as 'competitive doubles'. This would qualify for a double of $2\heartsuit$:

$\spadesuit$ J 8 $\heartsuit$ 9 4 3 $\diamondsuit$ A Q 8 4 $\clubsuit$ K 9 4 3

South doubles as a competitive move in spades or either minor. South intends to pass any minimum rebid by North.

$\spadesuit$ 8 $\heartsuit$ 9 4 $\diamondsuit$ A J 8 4 3 $\clubsuit$ K 9 7 4 3

South would double $2\heartsuit$ with this hand, too, but if North bids $2\spadesuit$, South rebids $3\clubsuit$, offering North the choice between $3\clubsuit$ and $3\diamondsuit$.

South's double of $2\clubsuit$ is also for takeout since it makes little sense to double a forcing bid for penalties. South's double here shows a willingness to compete in spades or diamonds. This would qualify:

$\spadesuit$ Q 8 $\heartsuit$ 9 4 $\diamondsuit$ A Q 8 4 3 $\clubsuit$ 10 8 6 2

West	North	East	South
1♣	No	1♡	1♠
Double . . .			

How do you interpret West's double? In days of yore it was a penalty double, following a principle that once partner has bid, all doubles are for penalties. That approach has merit, as there is no evidence that East-West have found a fit. However, the penalty double in this type of auction has been supplanted by another more fruitful use, whose popularity has grown with the advent of the LTT.

In the likely event that the auction becomes competitive, with East-West having a fit in hearts and North-South in spades, East will want to compete to the level indicated by the LTT, but East can be accurate here only if East knows how many hearts West holds.

Playing 'support doubles', West's double shows exactly three-card support for East's major suit. As a corollary, a 2♡ rebid by West would promise four-card support. Double = three trumps, raise = four trumps and other actions by West deny 3+ support for East's hearts.

West	North	East	South
1♣	No	1♡	Double
Redouble			

For similar reasons, players use the redouble here to show three-card support ('support redouble') and raising responder's major promises four trumps. Again this is considered more useful than a mere strength-showing redouble. If West fails to redouble or raise, the implication is that West holds less than three-card support.

A support double in the first auction above would be apt with:

(c) ♠ K J 4   ♡ Q 7 3   ◇ A Q   ♣ K Q 10 5 3

(d) ♠ 9 8   ♡ Q 5 4   ◇ A 9   ♣ A K Q J 5 3

(e) ♠ 9   ♡ 8 5 4   ◇ A J 9 5   ♣ A K 9 4 3

The support double can obviously be made on a large variety of hands with 3-card support and common sense is necessary as the auction progresses. What should West say with hands (c), (d), (e) in the following auction?

West	North	East	South
1♣	No	1♡	1♠
Double	No	2♡	No
?			

West must be aware that while East is quite likely to have five hearts for the 2♡ bid it is not guaranteed. For example, East might have:

♠ 7 6 3 2   ♡ A J 10 4   ◇ J 7 3   ♣ 7 2

With a third club East might have preferred 2♣ to 2♡, but with the actual hand, 2♡ is the most sensible choice.

With (c) West continues with 2NT, a natural game try.

With (d) West bids 3♣ to show strength and stress the club suit.

With (e) West passes. Any bid would be a game try. If East can do no more than 2♡, no further move by West is warranted.

Flexible Doubles In Crowded Auctions

By now you may be wondering whether any doubles of low-level suit contracts are for penalties. The answer is, 'not many'. It would be possible to write a lengthy book on this subject alone. A huge number of auctions can develop and it is obviously essential to know whether a double is for takeout or for penalties. The principles involved can be illustrated by considering various examples.

What should North do with this collection after the auction below:

♠ K Q 9 8   ♡ 6 4   ◇ A K J 10 8   ♣ A 5

West	North	East	South
1♡	Double	No	3♣
3♡	?		

West	North	East	South
1♡	Double	No	3♣
3♡	?		

♠ K Q 9 8   ♡ 6 4   ◇ A K J 10 8   ♣ A 5

With just your side vulnerable, you double West's 1♡ opening and plan to bid diamonds if partner does not bid spades. South gives you a pleasant surprise with a jump to 3♣. Your intention of changing suit to 3◇ (forcing, of course, because a hand too strong for a 2◇ overcall opposite a hand worth a jump to 3♣ is clearly worth game) is rudely shattered when West makes the annoying bid of 3♡. This seems to take little bidding space away but it is remarkably inconvenient. A sensible approach to such a problem is to consider your options and then pick the least flawed.

3♠ would suggest a single-suited hand with spades.

3NT would promise a heart stopper.

4♣ may leave you in the wrong denomination.

4◇ would describe your hand well enough, but it bypasses 3NT, which may be the correct contract.

Pass in no way describes your extra values. Partner could reasonably pass, too, leaving you with little compensation for a vulnerable game.

A penalty double would probably give you about 300, not adequate compensation for your vulnerable game.

None of these 'answers' solves the problem. That is why experts tend to play double here as showing extra values, a sort of 'card showing' takeout double. Partner can remove it or pass for penalties, as partner sees fit. You lose little by giving up the out-and-out penalty double. After all, having made a takeout double initially, how often will you find yourself sitting there with a heart stack? Of course, partner will not always make the right decision. However, when the auction becomes crowded, perfection can rarely be achieved. Accept that the opponents have made life hard for you and aim for a sensible result. A 'card showing' takeout double will rarely lead you astray.

West	North	East	South
1♠	4♢	?	

♠ A 6   ♡ Q J 9 5 4   ♢ 8   ♣ A Q 10 6 3

Vulnerable against not, you hold this fine hand and hear partner open 1♠. You are looking forward to a fruitful dialogue to determine which game or slam to bid when North curtails any discussion with a pre-emptive leap to 4♢. How do you cope with this?

It does not pay to reserve the double for those rare occasions when you want to penalise 4♢. This is a sensible rule: *After any opposition pre-empt, double is for takeout.* Double will produce a sensible rebid from your partner, who might have one of these:

(f) ♠ K Q 10 9 7 4   ♡ A 7   ♢ 7 4 2   ♣ K 5

(g) ♠ K J 9 7 4   ♡ A 8 7 6 2   ♢ 7   ♣ K 5

(h) ♠ K J 9 7 4   ♡ K 6   ♢ K 10 7   ♣ K 5 4

(i) ♠ K Q J 7 4   ♡ A 6 3 2   ♢ - - -   ♣ K 5 4 2

With (f), West will bid 4♠ after your double.

With (g), West will remove the double to 4♡.

With (h), West's diamonds are more useful in defence than offence and so West passes. A corollary to the above rule applies here: *After a high-level takeout double, remove the double only to a contract that you expect to make.* Partner will not remove the double with a hand like (h) when there is no obvious contract in your direction.

With (i), West bids 5♢. The hand is not strong in HCP but the void in the enemy suit boosts the ODR. Facing a penalty double, West would feel obliged to pass but opposite a takeout double at the four-level, suggesting game values, West can see the slam potential when holding just five losers. 6♡ or 6♣ is almost certain for East-West and, while thirteen tricks might be made, it is wise after a pre-empt to tread the conservative slam path unless you can see thirteen tricks.

West	North	East	South
1♠	No	2♣	4♡
?			

What should West do at red vulnerability with this hand:

♠ A Q J 9 5   ♡ 8   ◇ A J 10 6 5   ♣ A 7

Generally, the higher the pre-empt, the greater the need for takeout doubles. West has a better-than-minimum opening and opposite a two-level new suit response it is highly likely that a sound game would have been reached. What are West's rational options after South jams the bidding with 4♡?

West could bid 4♠ but that is unilateral. East might pass and you find yourself in a silly contract, with 5♣ or 5◇ makeable. 4♠ puts all your eggs in one basket.

West could bid 4NT, an interesting move. 4NT in a competitive auction such as this is neither Blackwood, nor natural (see Chapter 15 for more details). 4NT indicates a choice of contracts, and if the right spot is 5♣ or 5◇ then 4NT will undoubtedly find it. With spade support or preference, partner can opt for 5♠. The main drawback to 4NT is that if the last making contract is 4♠ you have just passed it.

West could bid 5◇. This could work but it is inferior to 4NT since it bypasses not just 4♠ but 5♣ as well. Essentially, 5◇ gives partner the choice of diamonds or spades and might already be too high. If clubs is where you should be, it is unlikely that you will reach it now.

West could pass. Some experts play that after a two-level change of suit the opponents should not be allowed to play in their contract undoubled. Pass does not begin to describe these values. How sure will you be that you are in the right contract if partner doubles 4♡?

The best action for West is a takeout double, inviting partner to bid if appropriate and pass with no attractive move. Double leaves all options open and caters for almost all contingencies. It allows partner to choose 4♠, 5♣ or 5◇ and if none of those appeals, partner can pass for penalties. It does not get much better than that.

Chapter 11

Defending against Pre-empts

Defending against the Weak Two-Opening

Weak twos, for which an opening two-level bid shows 5-9 HCP and a six-card suit, have all but replaced strong twos in popularity in tournament bridge. A six-card pre-empt is a good description of the standard weak two. However, when standards are slipping in so many walks of life, it is not surprising to find that it happens in bridge as well. Many pairs nowadays espouse weak two openings with just a five-card suit. They are prepared to sacrifice safety and accuracy in order to make life tough for the opposition.

The double of a weak two-bid is played almost universally for takeout. A 2NT overcall shows about 16-18 points. Bidding over that should follow almost the same paths as bidding after a 2NT opening, with Stayman and transfers in reply. Generally the criteria for intervening over a weak two-bid are similar to those after their one-level opening bid, but there are some differences.

Firstly, suit-overcalls at the cheapest level normally have opening hand values. A six-loser hand is expected for a three-level suit bid.

Secondly, jump-overcalls are strong, whatever methods you prefer over their one-level opening bids. A wide-ranging principle applies here. If an opponent's bid is weak, then your priority is to describe your strong hands. On the other hand if their bid is strong (e.g., a strong 1♣ opening) then your priority should be a disruptive bidding structure to make life hard for them. This advice can be summarised, *'Bid weakly over their strong bids and strongly over their weak bids'.*

If partner doubles, say, a weak 2♡ there is less space to describe your hand than if partner had doubled 1♡. A popular solution involves giving up the natural use of a 2NT response to the double and adapting the Lebensohl convention to help in this area.

West	North	East	South
2♡	Double	No	?

Using the Lebensohl convention, South's options include:

A two-level suit response (i.e., 2♠) shows 0-7 points.

A three-level suit response (i.e., 3♣ or 3♢) shows 8-10 points, constructive but not forcing. 3♠ shows 8-10 points and 5+ spades.

A 2NT response is a puppet, asking opener to bid 3♣. South can then show a weak by hand by passing or signing off in diamonds (showing 0-7 points in each case). South can continue with 3♠ (8-10 points and four spades) or, with enough for game, 3♡ (4 spades and no heart stopper) or 3NT (denying 4 spades and denying a heart stopper).

A 3♡ response is game-forcing with four spades and a heart stopper.

A 3NT response denies four spades but shows a heart stopper.

West	North	East	South
2♡	Double	No	2NT
No	?		

North is expected to bid 3♣ and should do so with any normal doubling hand. If North is exceptionally strong, (20 points or more, or fewer than five losers), bidding 3♣ is too risky as it may be passed. Any suit bid by North other than 3♣ implies around 20 points, about a 4-loser hand. It is not forcing but advancer should be keen to bid to game with one sure trick or better. With a rock-crusher worth game, North rejects 3♣ and bids 3♡, the enemy suit, to force to game.

Defending against the Weak Three-Bid

You need to adopt a philosophical and positive attitude when the opponents pre-empt. Any action is fraught with danger and you cannot crime yourself or, worse still, partner when a chosen action backfires and costs plenty. The risks are known: if you bid, you might be doubled and a substantial penalty might ensue if your hand does not mesh with partner's or if trumps break badly (as they are wont to do). However, there is no safety in passing when you have a decent hand, else you could miss a game or even a slam.

Suppose at game all RHO opens 3♠ and you are looking at:

♠ 9 4   ♡ K J 9 8 6 5   ◇ A K   ♣ K Q 3

Do you bid 4♡, or do you pass?

4♡ (doubled) will certainly be costly if partner has this hand:

♠ K 10 7 3   ♡ 2   ◇ J 9 7 5   ♣ 8 5 4 2

To make matters even worse, 3♠ would probably have failed.

However, you cannot live your life expecting lightning to strike you at every turn. Nothing ventured, nothing gained. If you pass and the layout is as shown below West will raise 3♠ to 4♠, which will make, while 5♡ is laydown for North-South. This is broadly in line with expectations from the LTT: 20 total trumps and 21 total tricks.

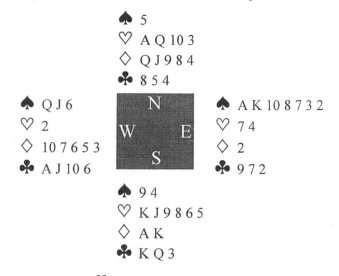

You should bid 4♡ and if you wish to feel stress and anxiety in the process, go right ahead. Worry if you will, but still bid 4♡. Your partnership must have sufficient maturity to recognise that South has a tough problem over 3♠, and whatever the outcome, recriminations are counter-productive. Have you noticed that partner does not play better after a rebuke? Right. A word to the wise is sufficient.

Take the pre-emptive opener to hold 8 HCP and the remaining strength to be divided evenly between the two unknown hands.

South: ♠ 9 4   ♡ K J 9 8 6 5   ◇ A K   ♣ K Q 3

After East opens 3♠, South reasons, 'I have 16 points. If East has 8, and the remaining 16 points are distributed evenly between West and North, partner will have 8 points. I have two spades. If East has seven, then West and North may have two each. I have six hearts. If East has a singleton, maybe West and North have three each.'

Put all that together and North-South are assumed to hold about 24 points with nine hearts, while East-West have 16 points and nine spades. With 18 total tricks it is correct for North-South to bid 4♡ rather than allow East-West to steal the contract in 3♠.

You assume partner has some values and take them into account. It is reasonable to play partner for two useful cards and bid accordingly. On the hand above, South has five losers. If North has the two tricks expected, the loser count drops to three and ten tricks are likely.

It follows that partner must not look rosily at ten useful points and argue that a slam try is justified since you expect to make ten tricks opposite garbage. You are not expecting garbage. You have already taken partner for two tricks and so partner needs significantly more than that before becoming slam-conscious.

After an opponent's pre-empt, generally be satisfied to play in a sensible contract. You rarely have enough room to investigate a slam without climbing too high. Borderline slams are best avoided since the pre-empt has warned you that suits are unlikely to break well.

Suppose, at game all your partner, South, overcalls East's 3♡ with 3♠. West passes. What should you bid as North with these hands?

(a) ♠ Q 8 4   ♡ K 8 4   ◇ Q J   ♣ Q 7 4 3 2

(b) ♠ Q 8 4   ♡ 4   ◇ A 10 9 5 4   ♣ 8 4 3 2

(c) ♠ Q 8 4   ♡ A 8 4   ◇ K J 4 3   ♣ 6 4 2

(d) ♠ Q 8 4   ♡ K Q 10   ◇ K 9 4 3   ♣ 6 4 2

As partner has assumed you have about two tricks, you should bid to game only if you exceed partner's expectations. With (a) you should pass. Your points are not particularly suitable for a spade contract. The ♠Q counts as one trick and a diamond ruff may be another. The ♡K is unlikely to contribute a trick.

Hand (b) is worth 4♠. Your ODR is far higher than with (a). The ♠Q and ◇A are your two expected tricks and you can count one more for the heart singleton. Also West did not raise to 4♡ even though West is sure to have some points. Therefore West will not have strong heart support and so South has some length in hearts, which in turn suggests that South does not have a minimum 3♠ overcall.

Hands (c) and (d) have the minimum trick capacity to justify bidding game. However, the texture of the hands is different. With (c) you raise to 4♠ and there is no strong case for any other choice.

Hand (d) looks similar, but you should appreciate that 4♠ will play less well than with hand (c). If partner has a singleton heart, your ♡K-Q-10 may be wasted. If West has a singleton, the defence will start with a heart to East's ace and a heart ruff. You might consider passing with (d), but a good shot, despite the risk in clubs, is 3NT.

How should you play double of a pre-empt? How often will you have a hand strong in their suit and how often short in their suit? The latter is far more frequent and doubling for takeout is more efficient than other methods. In the direct seat, double with slightly more than you might have for a double of a one-level opening. A six-loser hand is a good guide. In the pass-out seat you can double with one trick less, i.e., a seven-loser hand would be a sound minimum. The more cards you have in the pre-empt suit the more strength you need. These hands qualify as a minimum double of a 3◇ opening on your right:

(e) ♠ A 9 8 4 3   ♡ K 7 6 3   ◇ - - -   ♣ A 8 5 2

(f) ♠ A J 8 4   ♡ K Q 6 3   ◇ 7   ♣ A 8 5 2

(g) ♠ K Q 8 4   ♡ A K 4   ◇ 7 5   ♣ A 8 5 2

Shortage in their suit allows you to double on quite modest values.

West	North	East	South
3 ◇	Double	No	?

How is South to judge how high to bid? Be prepared to bid game with three winners or more. Partner is playing you for two tricks and so you need more than that. If partner has a six-loser minimum double, you need three tricks (for 4♡ or 4♠) to reduce the losers to three and so have a prospect for ten tricks.

What should South do with these hands after the above start?

(h) ♠ K J 8 4   ♡ Q 10 5   ◇ Q 8   ♣ J 8 4 3

(i) ♠ K J 8 4   ♡ Q 10 7 5   ◇ 8 2   ♣ K 4 3

(j) ♠ K J 8 4   ♡ Q 10 7 5   ◇ 8 2   ♣ A K 4

(k) ♠ K 9 3 2   ♡ 9 4 3   ◇ K 9 4   ♣ 8 6 2

(l) ♠ K 9 3 2   ♡ 9 4 3   ◇ A 9 4   ♣ A J 3

(m) ♠ 9 4 3   ♡ A 9 4   ◇ 9 5 4 3   ♣ A K 8

With (h), bid 3♠. You can count two tricks (♠K and ♡Q), no more.

With (i), you have enough for game but which major? To ask partner to choose the denomination, bid 4◇, their suit. Similar to the takeout double itself, a bid of the enemy suit expresses doubt as to the best contract. If you knew the right spot, you would bid it.

With (j), there is slam potential, but it is not easy to investigate this without committing yourself to the five-level, which might not be safe with bad breaks possible. You may bid beyond the safety of game if you feel there is a significantly greater chance of making a slam than of failing at the five-level. This is not mere percentages. Psychologically it can be very demoralising to go one down in a freely bid 5♡ or 5♠. With (j) it is sufficient to bid 4◇ and pass North's major suit rebid.

With (k) 3♠ is ample. It is false logic to say that as you have a diamond stopper you might as well try 3NT on the grounds that it is at the same level as 3♠. Playing 3NT with a combined 20 points and no fit is never much fun, and you might well be doubled.

With (l) 3NT and 4♠ are both sensible. How can you know which is better? No one can tell for sure, but if 4♠ is making, then 3NT is unlikely to be hopeless, whereas if 3NT is superior, playing 4♠ on a 4-3 fit (with a possible 5-1 trump break) might be not only hopeless but also doubled. ◇A-x-x is a very useful holding for 3NT. You can hold up with the ◇A and the pre-emptor may have no outside entry.

Hand (m) poses a different problem. There is no obvious fit, yet you have good values. To find the solution consider your ODR, which is not high, and try to estimate total tricks. It is quite likely that your opponents have eight diamonds, while your best fit is probably seven cards. With only 15 (or perhaps 16) total tricks, pass is the best option.

Of course you would not dream of passing a takeout double of 1◇ with this hand, but the higher the level the more often you pass a takeout double if you have a flat hand. This has implications for the doubler. Suppose RHO opens 3◇. What would you bid with this:

♠ A Q J 8 5 4 3   ♡ K Q 5   ◇ - - -   ♣ A J 2

You would double a 1◇ opening bid, with the intention of bidding spades strongly on the next round. There is only a tiny risk that partner will pass for penalties. You cannot afford to double 3◇ because the danger of partner passing is much greater. Best is to bid 4♠. Admittedly you might miss a good slam, but no action after a pre-empt is risk-free. Locating the right game takes priority.

West	North	East	South
3◇	Double	No	3♠
No	?		

What should North do with these cards:

♠ A J 3   ♡ A Q J 8   ◇ 9   ♣ A K J 10 4

'Seek the best game and let the slams take care of themselves' is sound strategy after a pre-empt. You want to be in game, but which game is best? Bid 4◇, meaning 'pick a game, any game'. It is more fruitful to use their suit here to express doubt as to the right contract than as a control bid suggesting slam in spades.

West	North	East	South
3♦	?		

What should North do with these hands?

(n)   ♠ A K J 9 3   ♡ A Q 10 6 5   ♦ 7   ♣ A 9

(o)   ♠ K 9 4 3 2   ♡ A Q 10 6 5   ♦ 7   ♣ A 9

The cue-bid of 4♦ is nowadays played as a Michaels Cue-Bid, showing both majors, rather than as a game-forcing takeout with a rock-crusher . You have no problem bidding 4♦ with a hand as strong as (n) but you have a tougher decision with (o). With (o) you could bid 3♡, 3♠ or 4♦, or you could double. In terms of values the hand is worth no more than a 3-level overcall, but which suit should West bid? To bid 3♡ or 3♠ could land in a misfit with a strong fit, and game, available in the other major.

The advantage of bidding 4♦ with (o) is that at least you will arrive in the correct denomination even if you play at the wrong level. That means that you will be in the correct game if there is one. Experts are prepared to stretch a level if the result is the correct strain. Hence the 4♦ cue-bid here can be an intermediate or a strong major two-suiter.

Double will probably also find the right major suit game, if there is one. If partner bids 3♡ or 3♠, you can raise, and if partner bids 3NT or 4♣, you can bid 4♦ to express doubt as to contract. The danger in doubling is that partner may choose 5♣, while an immediate 4♦ places the focus solely on the majors.

West	North	East	South
3♡	3NT . . .		

There are two hand types for 3NT here, firstly the balanced hands with a heart stopper in the range of 16-25 points. Note that there are many more balanced hands of 16 points than of 25 points, so partner with a balanced 9 points should not raise to 4NT: 'just in case you had 24-25, partner'. Secondly, there are hands which have a running minor suit and a guard in the enemy suit.

At equal or favourable vulnerability it would be reasonable to bid 3NT after their 3♡ opening with these hands:

(p)   ♠ 9 5   ♡ A 7   ◇ K 8   ♣ A K Q 7 5 4 3

(q)   ♠ A 8   ♡ K   ◇ Q 4 3   ♣ A K Q 7 5 4 3

Bidding 3NT with (q) is a calculated gamble but it will work far more often than you might expect. If a heart is led after RHO opened, there is every chance that with something like ♡A-Q-J-x-x-x-x and no outside entry, RHO will play the ♡J at trick 1.

If LHO opened 3♡ and you bid 3NT in fourth seat, this gambit is even more likely to work if opener's suit is A-Q-J-x-x-x-x or similar. LHO will hardly lead out the ♡A and on a lower heart lead, you scamper home with nine tricks if the clubs behave. Of course, if you play with fire you may sometimes be burned. LHO's suit may not be ace-high suit and a low heart may be led to the ace on your right. If disaster does strike, hopefully you and partner can maintain at least a facade of cheerfulness.

Defending against Four-Level Opening Bids

A double of a four-level opening bid was used traditionally merely with a strong hand. Shortage in their suit was possible but a strong balanced hand was equally likely. This makes judgement difficult.

Modern style is to play doubles of four-level pre-empts for takeout. The doubler should have a good hand with shortage in the suit opened and support for the unbid suits. The doubler's partner should imagine the doubler to hold a strong 4-4-4-1, with the singleton in the suit opened, and act accordingly.

West	North	East	South
4♡	Double	No	?

What should South do with these hands?

(r)   ♠ 9 5 4 2   ♡ 8 5 4   ◇ 9 5 4 3 2   ♣ 3

(s)   ♠ K 8   ♡ 7   ◇ Q J 7 5 2   ♣ Q 9 8 6 3

(r) ♠ 9 5 4 2   ♡ 8 5 4   ◇ 9 5 4 3 2   ♣ 3

With (r), pass is best. Of course, 4♡ doubled might make but if so, the likely penalty in 4♠ or 5◇ doubled will be horrendous. Passing will not automatically lead to a minus score. Partner might have enough in hand to defeat 4♡ or you might aid the cause with some club ruffs.

(s) ♠ K 8   ♡ 7   ◇ Q J 7 5 2   ♣ Q 9 8 6 3

With (s), bid 4NT. You are likely to have a fit in both minors but you may as well play in the better combined suit. 4NT is a form of the Unusual No-Trump. It shows that East has at least two playable spots, in this case clearly the minors because the 4NT bid has bypassed 4♠.

You can also bid 4NT at once to show a pronounced two-suiter. Each of these would be suitable at favourable or equal vulnerability after RHO opens 4♡.

(t) ♠ 6   ♡ 8   ◇ K Q 10 8 6   ♣ Q J 10 7 4 3

(u) ♠ 6   ♡ 8   ◇ A K Q 10 8   ♣ A Q J 9 7 2

(v) ♠ - - -   ♡ A 6 4   ◇ K 10 6 5 2   ♣ A J 7 4 3

With (t) you bid 4NT in the hope of finding a cheap save, or perhaps tempting LHO into bidding 5♡. With (u) you expect to make game in whichever minor partner chooses. The important feature is the very high ODR in each case.

It may surprise you that 4NT is sensible with the modest values in hand (v). It is much safer than it might appear because of your heart holding. Partner figures to be short in hearts and therefore is likely to have length in at least one of the minors. It pays to take that chance.

A double of 4♠ was traditionally made on a strong balanced hand. Again this style has changed among many experts who prefer to use the double purely on takeout shape, shortage in their suit, support for the other suits. Again, frequency is a relevant consideration. After a 4♠ opening, are you likely to have length in spades or shortage? You do not give up on penalties, as partner may elect to pass the double.

Playing double as takeout, the double tends to be three-suited and 4NT can still be used for the freakish two-suiter.

WEST	EAST	Dealer South : Any vulnerability			
♠ - - -	♠ 10 7 4 2	West	North	East	South
♡ A Q J 10 4	♡ K 6 5 2				4♠
◇ K J 10 9 6 2	◇ Q 5	4NT	No	5♣	No
♣ 8 2	♣ K Q 6	5◇	No	5♡	All pass

4NT shows any two-suiter. East bids 5♣ in case West holds the minors. The removal to 5◇ shows diamonds and hearts.

This arose in the 2000 Olympiad Open Teams (Austria vs Brazil):

Dealer South : Nil vulnerable

♠ Q J 10 9 5 4 3
♡ A 9 8 2
◇ A
♣ 9

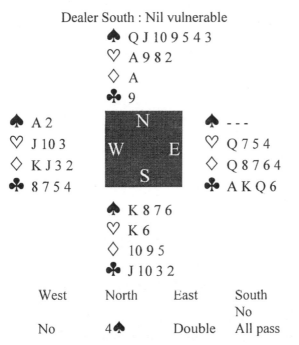

♠ A 2
♡ J 10 3
◇ K J 3 2
♣ 8 7 5 4

♠ - - -
♡ Q 7 5 4
◇ Q 8 7 6 4
♣ A K Q 6

♠ K 8 7 6
♡ K 6
◇ 10 9 5
♣ J 10 3 2

West	North	East	South
			No
No	4♠	Double	All pass

North made eleven tricks for +690. At the other table North's 4♠ was passed out, +450. West should not pass the double. With a fit in two suits, 4NT was the move and East would bid 5◇. Whatever happens thereafter will be better than 4♠ doubled. The message should be clear: *Without length in their suit, take out takeout doubles.*

Chapter 12

High-Level Competitive Auctions

The higher the standard at which you play, the more competition you can expect. Experts have two, seemingly contradictory, sayings. Firstly there is: 'When in doubt, bid one more'. Suppose you have a spade fit while your opponents have a heart fit and both sides are vulnerable. The bidding has reached 4♡. Should you bid 4♠?

Maybe you have the feeling that both contracts will go one off. In that case bidding 4♠ will turn +100 into −100 (or −200 if you are doubled). However suppose you are slightly wrong, so that they can make 4♡ while you are only one off in 4♠. In that case, bidding 4♠ reduces −620 to −100 (or −200 if you are doubled). It is worth stressing that if you do bid 4♠ occasionally your opponents will persevere to 5♡, and in that case your 4♠ has turned −620 into +100. Remember, your opponents find these high-level decisions as difficult as you do. There is much to be said for putting them under pressure and letting them make the last mistake.

The second saying is: 'The five-level belongs to your opponents'. Consider this auction:

West	North	East	South
1♡	1♠	4♡	4♠
5♡	?		

In considering whether to bid 5♠, North should bear in mind that South may have taken a considerable risk in bidding 4♠, and that South might have already done very well by pushing the opponents from a laydown 4♡ to a doomed 5♡. In that case North will undo all of South's good work if North continues to 5♠ and fails. Generally speaking, if they wanted to play at the four-level and your side has succeeded in pushing them to the five-level you have done well and you should let matters rest, unless you are virtually certain your contract will succeed.

Of course these sayings are just guide-lines and are no substitute for intelligent judgement. In competitive auctions in which you have found a fit you should try to apply the LTT and the Losing Trick Count, with consideration given to your ODR.

West	North	East	South
1♠	2♦	4♠	?

What should South do at game all with these hands:

(a)   ♠ 3   ♡ K Q J 5   ◇ K J 10 4   ♣ 9 5 3 2

(b)   ♠ 3 2   ♡ K Q J 5   ◇ K J 10 4   ♣ 9 5 3

(c)   ♠ 9 3 2   ♡ K Q J 5   ◇ K J 10 4   ♣ 9 5

(d)   ♠ K   ♡ A 8 7 5   ◇ A 10 9 4   ♣ 9 5 3 2

(e)   ♠ A 9 4   ♡ A 8 3 2   ◇ Q J 10 8   ♣ 8 7

(f)   ♠ Q J 10   ♡ A 8 3 2   ◇ A 10 9 4   ♣ 8 7

The points seem to be distributed roughly 50-50. How about total tricks? It is likely that North has six diamonds when East holds two or three diamond honours. To overcall 2♦ with minimum values and only a moderate 5-card suit would not be attractive when vulnerable.

North-South almost certainly have a 9-card fit, otherwise they would not be bidding so high with only half of the points in the pack. In particular, North, who has few points, figures to have five spades.

There are likely to be 19 or 20 total trumps. That suggests you should bid on unless your ODR indicates otherwise.

Hand (a) has a high ODR with a concentration of values in the heart suit and good intermediate diamonds. Bid 5♦.

Hand (b) has slightly poorer ODR because of the doubleton spade. The more balanced your hand, the lower your ODR. A doubleton in their suit is the worst holding for offence because of the danger that they can take the first two tricks. You have a close decision here between pass and 5♦, but choose 5♦ as they may push on to 5♠.

(c) ♠ 9 3 2   ♡ K Q J 5   ◇ K J 10 4   ♣ 9 5

Hand (c) seems to have a similar ODR to (b), but this time there is a good chance that partner has a singleton spade so the hand should play better in a diamond contract. Bid 5 ◇.

(d) ♠ K   ♡ A 8 7 5   ◇ A 10 9 4   ♣ 9 5 3 2

Hand (d) has a poor ODR. The red suit aces are neutral, while your singleton ♠K is a defensive value, maybe scoring on a finesse if they play 4♠ but doomed if visible in dummy. Pass is the percentage call.

(e) ♠ A 9 4   ♡ A 8 3 2   ◇ Q J 10 8   ♣ 8 7

Hand (e) has a reasonable ODR. Your spade holding opposite a singleton means no spade losers in 5 ◇. Certainly your diamond holding will be wasted defending 4♠. Bid 5 ◇.

(f) ♠ Q J 10   ♡ A 8 3 2   ◇ A 10 9 4   ♣ 8 7

Finally, hand (f) has a poor ODR. Again the red suit aces are neutral, but your spade holding strongly suggests defence. ♠Q-J-10 is a certain defensive trick, but it is likely to be totally wasted opposite a singleton spade in a 5 ◇ contract. Double 4♠.

The Slam Zone

The advice in Chapter 11, that it can be wise to settle for the best game, applies equally whether an opponent pre-empts with an opening bid or with an overcall, since there is very little room to investigate a slam in either case. Suppose you pick up as West:

♠ K 9 5 4   ♡ A Q J 8 7   ◇ A Q 9   ♣ 2

Do you bid 6♡ or pass after this bidding:

West	North	East	South
1♡	5♣	5♡	No
?			

Your hand has many attractive features including a control in every side suit, two aces and good trumps. 6♡ may well be laydown.

Indeed, if East expects to make eleven tricks opposite a minimum opening bid your hand should surely provide the twelfth. The trouble is that East does not necessarily expect to make eleven tricks if you are minimum. East has bid under pressure. East may hold something like this, which does make 6♡ laydown:

♠ A Q J 6 2   ♡ K 9 6 5   ◇ K J   ♣ 8 5

Equally East might have hand like this, when it will take every bit of your extra values, together with an ounce of luck, to make even 5♡:

♠ Q J 6 2   ♡ K 10 9 4 3 2   ◇ 5 4   ♣ 8

If your partner has courageously ventured 5♡ on these cards, you will undo all the good work if you bid 6♡. Not surprisingly, the result will be that your partner will be less inclined to compete in future. Never punish partner for showing enterprise. Be grateful that you have such a partner.

West	North	East	South
4♠	Double	No	?

What should South do with:

♠ 3   ♡ A Q 2   ◇ Q J 10 7 6 2   ♣ Q 10 9

Perhaps 6◇ is on but that is pure speculation. Do not let yourself be goaded into what might be a hopeless slam. Settle for a sensible 5◇.

What should South do with the same cards if the bidding goes:

West	North	East	South
4♠	Double	5♠	?

This time the choice is between +300 or +500 if you double, and either +1370 or −100 if you bid 6◇. You no longer have the option of +600 for making 5◇.

If you expect that 6◇ will make about 50% of the time, then your score expectation is +1370 − 100 divided by two, i.e., a bit above +600. On that basis, it is worth trying 6◇. In addition, even if your slam is failing, the opponents might sacrifice in 6♠.

West	North	East	South
1♡	1♠	4♡	No
?			

What should West do with:

♠ 7 6 4 3　　♡ A Q 10 9 3 2　　♢ - - -　　♣ A Q J

It would be unsound to move further after partner's pre-emptive raise to 4♡. Even 5♡ may not be safe.

What should West do with the same cards if the bidding has been:

West	North	East	South
1♡	1♠	4♡	4♠
?			

This makes a huge difference. South's 4♠ virtually guarantees that East has a singleton or perhaps a void in spades. The opposition bidding indicates you have a miracle fit. A slam should be at worst on the club finesse, and may be laydown. Go ahead and bid the slam.

As long as there is no scope for partnership misunderstanding, a thoughtful West would jump to 6♢ as a lead-directing move en route to 6♡. Of course North will convert this to 6♡, but if they sacrifice in 6♠ doubled, a diamond lead from partner will be a welcome start.

The Forcing Pass

West	North	East	South
		1♣	No
2♠	4♡	4♠	6♡
6♠	No	No	7♡
?			

What should West do, with only East-West vulnerable, holding:

♠ A K J 10 8 6　　♡ - - -　　♢ K 10 8 7　　♣ K J 6

You were content to play in 6♠, but now the choice is between trying for the grand slam or taking a penalty from 7♡. Doubling 7♡ is unlikely to provide sufficient compensation for your vulnerable slam but that will be better than bidding 7♠ and failing. There are two courses of action, but you have three choices of call.

You can double to warn partner against bidding further. That will end the auction. You would definitely double if you had a losing heart. You can bid 7♠, taking the risk that the ♣A or ♢A may be missing.

These two calls are unilateral, in that you are trying to make the final decision on your own. The other option is to pass and involve partner in the decision-making. If you pass, it is inconceivable that partner will also pass. Your bidding has clearly indicated that your side holds the majority of high cards and that your opponents are the ones who are sacrificing.

Your pass is a *forcing pass*. That means partner is required to bid further or to double their contract. Here it shows interest in 7♠ and promises first-round control in their suit, hearts. The pass asks partner to judge whether the assets held seem suitable for a grand slam in the light of the bidding to date. What should East do with:

(g) ♠ Q 7 3   ♡ 10 4   ♢ A 5   ♣ A Q 10 4 3 2

(h) ♠ Q 7 3   ♡ K 9   ♢ Q 5   ♣ A Q 10 4 3 2

With (g), East will bid 7♠ because although the hand is minimum all the high cards seem to be working. However with (h), East will double 7♡, because the ♡K is wasted in a spade contract and while (h) has more points than (g), its ODR is lower than for hand (g).

Slam-Sacrifice Doubles

In the auction opposite, South took a save in 7♡. It would have been unfortunate to play in 7♡ doubled if it were possible to defeat 6♠. Sometimes each partner might have one defensive trick but neither is aware of the defensive potential held by the other. This scheme gives you a method of reducing the incidence of the 'phantom sacrifice':

West	North	East	South
1♦	3♥	Double	4♥
5♣	No	6♣	?

East's double was for takeout and the opponents have bid freely to a slam. It may pay East-West to save in 6♥, especially at favourable vulnerability, but not if 6♣ can be defeated. The rules are:

In the direct seat (South):
Double = 2 defensive tricks. Pass = 0 or 1 defensive trick.

In the pass-out seat (North after No bid, No bid):
If partner has doubled (2 defensive tricks), you pass.
If partner has passed (0 or 1 trick):
  Pass with 2 defensive tricks.
  Double with 1 defensive trick.
  Sacrifice with 0 defensive tricks.

West	North	East	South
1♦	3♥	Double	4♥
5♣	No	6♣	No
No	Double	No	?

After the player in the pass-out seat has doubled (1 defensive trick), the partner will pass with one defensive trick, too, and sacrifice with no defensive trick.

Naturally you have to decide what counts as a defensive trick. You may not always be right with these decisions but it is better to have some method here than none. In borderline cases, do not be anxious to sacrifice if the opponents have been pressured into a slam, but tend to trust vulnerable opponents who bid slam voluntarily.

The idea can be adapted for a sacrifice against a grand slam:

Direct seat: Double with 1 defensive trick, pass with 0 tricks or with potential for a trick.

Pass-out seat: If partner has doubled, you pass. If partner has passed, pass with 1 trick, sacrifice with 0 and double with potential for a trick. Partner will then sacrifice with 0 and pass with some potential.

In the examples so far, it has been abundantly clear which side had the overwhelming balance of strength and which side was sacrificing. Sometimes the situation is murky and even top class partnerships have misunderstandings whether or not a pass is forcing. It would be helpful to have a rule that determined beyond doubt when a pass is forcing. To pinpoint such a rule is not easy, but a good principle is: *If you have bid a game or slam with the expectation of making it, the enemy should not be allowed to outbid you and play undoubled.*

Here are some more guide-lines:

West	North	East	South		West	North	East	South
1♡	1♠	4♡	4♠		3♡	No	4♡	Double
No	No	?			No	4♠	No	No
					?			

If your partnership has bid only one suit and at least one of the bids was a pre-empt, then forcing passes do not apply. On that basis 4♠ may be passed out in each of the above auctions.

West	North	East	South		West	North	East	South
1♡	1♠	4♡	4♠		1♢	3♠	4♡	4♠
5♡	No	No	?		No	No	?	

If the four-level game-bid was the cheapest available bid in that suit over an opposing jump-bid then subsequent passes are not forcing. In each of these auctions, you might have a strong hand for your four-level bid but you might have done the same with quite modest values. If appropriate, partner would have doubled or bid on but otherwise, as only you know how strong a hand you have, partner has passed the decision to you to decide whether to bid on, pass or double. Pass is definitely an option.

Other than the foregoing, if your side has bid more than one suit and has bid to game, pass by either partner should be played as forcing. Of course you are free to choose different guide-lines when a pass is forcing. Vulnerability can be a criterion. All that really matters is that you and your partner agree!

Chapter 13

The Fit in Two Suits

(a)

    ♠ 9 6
    ♡ K 10 9 7
    ◇ A Q 10 6 5
    ♣ 3 2

♠ A K J 10 8      ♠ Q 7 5 2
♡ 3 2   ♡ 8 5
◇ 7 4   ◇ 3 2
♣ K J 9 8   ♣ A Q 10 6 5

    ♠ 4 3
    ♡ A Q J 6 4
    ◇ K J 9 8
    ♣ 7 4

How does the LTT work out on the deal above and the one below?

(b)

    ♠ 9 6 4
    ♡ K 10 9 7
    ◇ A Q 10 6 5
    ♣ 3

♠ A K J 10 8   N   ♠ Q 7 5 2
♡ 3   W   E   ♡ 8 5 2
◇ 7 4 2   S   ◇ 3
♣ K J 9 8   ♣ A Q 10 6 5

    ♠ 3
    ♡ A Q J 6 4
    ◇ K J 9 8
    ♣ 7 4 2

With North-South playing in hearts and East-West in spades, there are eighteen total trumps in each case. For deal (a), with each side having four losers, there are also eighteen total tricks.

The changes in (b) are tiny, but the effect dramatic. Suddenly, although the total number of trumps is still eighteen, there are twenty-two total tricks, North-South making 5♡ while East-West make 5♠.

Part of the reason that there are so many total tricks is that the hands have become more unbalanced. Even taking that into account the change in the total number of tricks is remarkable.

Now look at layout (c) below, the same as (b) but with the minor suits of North and East swapped. There are still eighteen total trumps. Would you care to estimate out the total number of tricks?

(c)

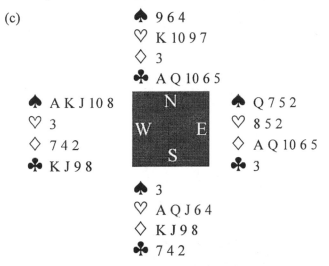

North:
♠ 9 6 4
♡ K 10 9 7
♢ 3
♣ A Q 10 6 5

West:
♠ A K J 10 8
♡ 3
♢ 7 4 2
♣ K J 9 8

East:
♠ Q 7 5 2
♡ 8 5 2
♢ A Q 10 6 5
♣ 3

South:
♠ 3
♡ A Q J 6 4
♢ K J 9 8
♣ 7 4 2

The play will be messy and it is not easy to work out the total number of tricks. Thanks to the layout of the minor suits, North-South can make ten tricks in hearts while repeated trump leads can hold East-West to eight tricks in spades: a total of eighteen total tricks.

The precise numbers are not so important. The point is that like (b) the hands are unbalanced, but now the total number of tricks has fallen dramatically. How do you account for that?

The great difference between (b) and (c) is that in (b) each side has a fit in a second suit while in (c) the minor suits fit badly. If you can diagnose that your side has a fit in two suits, then the consequence is that your opponents also have a fit in two suits, and so there will be more total tricks available than would be suggested by the LTT.

It is worthwhile considering how the auctions might develop for (b) and (c) with South as dealer and both sides vulnerable. With no conventional gadgets, the bidding is likely to start:

South	West	North	East
1♡	1♠	4♡	4♠ ...

Note that neither side discovers whether a fit in a second suit exists and so the final resting place is largely random. There is a better way to deal with these hands and this will be revealed a little later.

The following deal from a British tournament shows that even without conventional aids a fit in two suits can be diagnosed:

Dealer West : Nil vulnerable

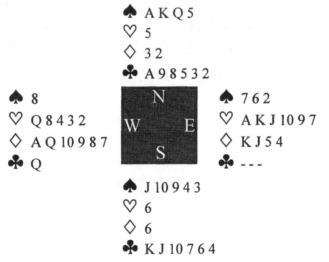

West generally passed because with such a minimum a 1♢ opening may leave West unable to show the hearts at all, while to open 1♡ and rebid 2♢ hardly suggests six good diamonds and five poor hearts.

Whatever the start to the auction, North-South will quickly find a club fit and East-West a heart fit. Whether they realise their full potential will depend on which side, if either, discovers the secondary fit. This auction seems reasonable:

West	North	East	South
No	1♣	1♡	5♣ (1)
5♢ (2)	5♠ (3)	6♢	6♠ (4)
No	No	Dble (5)	All pass

(1) 1♠ is a reasonable alternative, though there is a lot to be said for putting the pressure on East-West with a violent pre-empt.

(2) 5♢ is a thoughtful bid which shows diamonds *and* hearts. Having passed as dealer West would hardly venture in at the five-level opposite a simple overcall without a heart fit as well as the diamonds.

(3) North is going to bid 6♣, but 5♠ on the way achieves two objectives. Firstly, it asks for a spade lead if East buys the contract in 6♡ (doubled). Secondly, it might help South to diagnose a secondary spade fit.

(4) Without North's illuminating 5♠, South would pass at this point, and presumably North would double. 6♢ or 6♡ doubled and made was a common result. As it is South takes out insurance in 6♠, a very wise decision.

(5) East cannot feel certain of defeating 6♠, but no doubt feels rather frustrated at being outbid.

The result is par for the hand: 6♠, doubled and one or two down (depending on whether East scores the club ruff). That is good bridge. Each side has bid to its full potential, while neither has been pushed overboard.

Fit-Jumps

Fit-jumps are a way of diagnosing whether or not your side has a double fit. It is the best type of convention, in that it is an aid to judgement that occurs quite frequently rather than a fancy gadget that turns up only once in a blue moon.

The fit-jump fulfils two objectives that are vital to good competitive judgement. Firstly, it immediately describes your fit with partner's suit. Secondly, it announces a second suit, which will enable partner to see how well or badly the secondary suits fit.

In any a competitive auction, once your partner has bid a suit any jump in an unbid suit by you shows that suit, and good support for partner's suit.

(b)

	♠ 9 6 4	
	♡ K 10 9 7	
	◇ A Q 10 6 5	
	♣ 3	

♠ A K J 10 8	N	♠ Q 7 5 2
♡ 3	W E	♡ 8 5 2
◇ 7 4 2	S	◇ 3
♣ K J 9 8		♣ A Q 10 6 5

	♠ 3	
	♡ A Q J 6 4	
	◇ K J 9 8	
	♣ 7 4 2	

South	West	North	East
1♡	1♠	4◇	4♠
5♡	?		

This sequence puts North-South in a very strong position. North's fit-jump to 4◇ shows a hand worth a raise to 4♡ with a good diamond suit. That knowledge enables South to bid on over 4♠. South chooses 5♡ rather than 5◇ to mask the double fit as far as possible. To bid 5◇ would alert them to their own double fit.

Had North jumped to 4♣ instead, showing a heart fit and a club suit, South might double 4♠. The 4♣ fit-jump warns South against bidding higher. South would prefer a singleton club but even with rag clubs South wants to defend. The double tells North not to bid further.

Any jump in a new suit in a competitive auction should be a fit-jump.

West	North	East	South		West	North	East	South
1♡	1♠	3♣ ...			1♡	Dble	3♣ ...	

In the above auctions East is announcing a hand worth a raise to 3♡ with a club suit as well.

West	North	East	South		West	North	East	South
1♡	1♠	4♣ ...			1♡	Dble	4♣ ...	

This time East has shown a hand worth 4♡ with a club suit as well.

To justify the jump to 4♣ over 1♠, East might have (d) or (e) below but not (f):

(d)   ♠ 9 6   ♡ K J 8 4   ◇ 8 5   ♣ A Q J 9 8

(e)   ♠ 9   ♡ K 9 8 5 4   ◇ 8 5   ♣ Q J 10 8 2

(f)   ♠ Q 7   ♡ K 10 7 5   ◇ K 9   ♣ A 7 4 3 2

The point is that (d) and (e) have a high ODR, while (f) has a low ODR. The fit-jump promises good offensive values in the second suit. With a singleton in that suit, partner will diagnose wasted values. That would be correct opposite (d) or (e), but not opposite (f).

West	North	East	South
1♡	1♠	4♣	4♠
?			

If East can have either (d) or (e) for the 4♣ response, how can West tell what to do after South competes to 4♠ if West has this:

♠ 7   ♡ A Q 10 7 2   ◇ A 6 3   ♣ K 6 5 4

The answer is that it is correct for West to bid 5♡ whether East has hand (d) or hand (e). If East has (d) 5♡ is laydown (unless there is a club ruff going). If East has (e) 5♡ will fail by one trick, but that scarcely matters. 4♠ is laydown for North-South.

West bids 5♡ regardless, because West knows that the total number of tricks has been boosted by the double fit. Whichever contract happens to be making, bidding 5♡ will normally produce the best result for East-West.

West	North	East	South
1♡	1♠	4♣	4♠
?			

Now suppose that West has these cards after the same start:

♠ 7   ♡ A Q 10 7 2   ◇ A K 3   ♣ K 6 5 4

West will be aware that 6♡ would be an excellent contract opposite hand (d), while 5♡ will be quite high enough opposite (e). In this auction South can make a slam try with 5◇. Partner will bid 6♡ with (d) and sign off in 5♡ with (e).

In other auctions there might not be a convenient slam try. In that case South should be cautious about committing North-South to a slam. As always, the priority in the competitive auction is to find the right action at the four- or five-level, not to bid borderline slams. The occasional missed slam is a price you should be willing to pay if you can make better decisions in the sacrifice zone.

Finally, you will note that if you play 4♣ in the various sequences on page 111 and above as a fit-jump, then it cannot also be used as a splinter bid. Some pairs are very keen on splinter bids.

A compromise is to play that a single jump in a competitive auction is a fit-jump, such as a jump to 3♣ after 1♡ from partner and 1♠ by RHO, while a double jump, such as 4♣, is a splinter. That is perfectly playable and the ramifications should be a matter for partnership discussion. One corollary is that a fit-jump to the three-level shows enough to compete to that level but might have more.

Chapter 14

Defence to Artificial Bids

Defending against their Strong 1♣

No doubt you will from time to time find yourself playing against pairs who play Precision Club, Blue Club or Nottingham Club systems. They are based on the principle that almost all strong hands (16+ points) are opened with a forcing 1♣. With a weak hand (usually below 8 HCP) responder bids a negative 1◇. All other responses to 1♣ are forcing to game.

To deal effectively against these systems it is important to understand their strengths and weaknesses. The main strength is that if you can force to game with as cheap a sequence as 1♣ : (No) : 1♡ you have plenty of space to compare notes. The main weakness comes when opponents pre-empt, leaving opener to start describing the hand at an uncomfortably high level.

Your defence should be based on the principle stated in Chapter 11: *Bid weakly over their strong bids and strongly over their weak bids.* If you bid immediately over their 1♣ it should show a weak hand with the desire to interfere with their scientific bidding. How weak will depend on partnership preference, but common sense dictates that you clearly should not risk a huge penalty if vulnerable.

Over a 1♣ opening, or after (1♣) : No : (1◇), the following system of two-suited overcalls and weak jump-overcalls is called 'Truscott':

Jump-overcalls are natural, one-suited and weak.

A simple suit overcall shows a weak two-suiter, with the suit bid and the one above it. Thus, after 1♣:

1◇ = diamonds and hearts
1♡ = hearts and spades
1♠ = spades and clubs
2♣ = clubs and diamonds

The same style applies after (1♣) : No : (1♢) : ?

1♡ = hearts and spades
1♠ = spades and clubs
2♣ = clubs and diamonds
2♢ = diamonds and hearts

Jump-overcalls are weak one-suiters.

Double shows the suit doubled and the non-touching suit:

(1♣) : Double = clubs and hearts
(1♣) : No : (1♢) : Double = diamonds and spades

A 1NT overcall shows the other pair of non-touching suits:

(1♣) : 1NT = diamonds and spades
(1♣) : No : (1♢) : 1NT = clubs and hearts.

WEST	EAST	Dealer South : N-S vulnerable			
♠ 8 7 3	♠ 5	West	North	East	South
♡ Q J 10 4	♡ K 6				1♣
♢ K Q 9 7 6	♢ J 8 7 4 3 2	1♢	No	5♢...	
♣ 4	♣ 9 8 6 2				

West's hand, with its very high ODR, is ideal for the two-suited 1♢ overcall, which shows the red suits. With fewer than eight points North passes. East can see that North-South have a huge spade fit and could well have a spade slam. East pre-empts to the level suggested by the law of total tricks. Note that West is likely to lose just 300 if doubled in 5♢, while North-South should be able to make 6♣ or 6♠.

What if you have a strong hand after a strong 1♣ opening? The answer is, you pass. You are sure to have another opportunity and by the next round your opponents will have made a natural bid. If you wish to bid, you can now defend against this natural bid as if it were an opening bid. Having passed, all your later actions are strong.

West	North	East	South	West	North	East	South
1♣	No	1♢	No	1♣	No	1♢	No
1♡	2♠...			1♡	2♡...		
2♠ is a strong jump-overcall.				2♡ is Michaels, (strong variety).			

The effectiveness of the 'Multi 2◇' depends on opponents being unprepared. The main theory of the bid is that 2◇ shows either a weak two-bid in a major suit, or a strong hand. Nine times out of ten it will be the weak hand, so you should bid with strong hands immediately over 2◇.

The defence comes in two parts:

1. *In the direct seat* (after RHO has opened 2◇)

Suit bids at the cheapest level are natural, 16-19 points.

A suit jump-bid shows 19-22 and a good 6-card suit.

2NT = 19-21 points, balanced with guards in both major suits. Respond as though partner had opened 2NT.

3NT = 22-24 balanced.

All other hands of 16+ points start with a double.

If your partner doubles a multi 2◇ opening you should use the Lebensohl principle, just as over a weak 2♡ opening as described in chapter 11. There are many possibilities, depending on whether the third hand bids over the double, too many to list but here is a sample:

WEST	EAST	West	North	East	South
♠ A K 9 7	♠ 8 5				2◇
♡ 9	♡ 8 5 4 3	Dble	No	2NT	No
◇ A K Q 4	◇ 6 5	3♠	No	4♣	No
♣ A J 10 8	♣ Q 9 7 6 2	5♣	No	No	No

Double shows a strong hand but no convenient natural bid. West cannot tell for certain whether South has a weak two in hearts or in spades. 2NT asks West to bid 3♣ (East is planning to pass 3♣ but could have been intending to continue with 3♡ or 3♠ to show four cards in that suit but deny a stopper in the other major). West is too strong to accept a sign-off in clubs and shows this by refusing to accept the puppet to 3♣ and bidding 3♠ instead. 4♣ shows that East intended to sign off in 3♣ and West makes a sporting raise to game.

2. After the sequence $(2\diamondsuit)$: No : $(2\heartsuit)$: No; (No) : ?

$2\heartsuit$ asks opener to pass with a weak two in hearts or correct to $2\spadesuit$ with a weak two in spades. This is known as a 'pass or correct' bid.

When opener passes $2\heartsuit$, you know that opener has a weak two in hearts, so your defence is now the same as though the opening bid had been $2\heartsuit$. The only difference is that because you passed on the first round you are known not to have a strong hand.

If opener's rebid is $2\spadesuit$ you would play your defence to a weak $2\spadesuit$. However, all actions over $2\spadesuit$ will be below 16 points since you did not take immediate action over $2\diamondsuit$.

It may seem risky to bid with a modest hand but the logic of the auction makes it safe enough. RHO has a weak two opening and LHO could not rake up more than a weak, droppable response.

Apply a little logic and you should be able to handle any multi-$2\diamondsuit$ sequence. Suppose the bidding has been:

West	North	East	South
$2\diamondsuit$	No	$2\spadesuit$	No
$3\heartsuit$	No	$4\heartsuit$	?

What would you do with these South cards:

$\spadesuit$ J 9 5 4 3 $\heartsuit$ - - - $\diamondsuit$ A Q 6 3 $\clubsuit$ K 8 6 2

Many players would pass without a thought but consider the bidding. $2\spadesuit$ instructs West to pass with a weak two in spades or correct to $3\heartsuit$ with a weak two in hearts. Upon hearing of a weak $2\heartsuit$ opposite, East raises to $4\heartsuit$. Obviously East likes hearts far more than spades. It sounds as though East-West have a 9- or 10-card heart fit and you have a similar fit in spades. South should bid $4\spadesuit$, with the knowledge that North must have a good spade holding.

Action by the Fourth Hand

Suppose the bidding has started $(2\diamondsuit)$: No : $(2\heartsuit)$: ? If opener has a weak $2\heartsuit$ opening bid you will not get another chance. Therefore treat the $2\heartsuit$ bid as the opening and use your defence to a weak $2\heartsuit$.

Chapter 15

Other Conventional Gadgets

4NT and 5NT in Competition

Chapter 7 illustrated the Unusual No-trump over an enemy opening bid. Chapter 11 examined the use of 4NT over an enemy pre-empt. These are specific examples of a wide-ranging principle, namely that in competitive auctions, 4NT is normally not natural or Blackwood but is for takeout, usually suggesting that the bidder can see at least two possible final denominations.

West	North	East	South
1♣	4♠	No	No
4NT . . .			

4NT does not make sense as Blackwood opposite a passing partner. With clubs and hearts, West would re-open with a double. 4NT shows a freakish hand with the minors, perhaps something like this:

♠ 9   ♡ 7   ◇ K Q J 7 2   ♣ A Q J 6 5 3

West	North	East	South
1◇	4♠	No	No
4NT . . .			

West has diamonds and another suit. A 5♣ bid by West would have suggested a 5-5 pattern. If West's second suit is clubs, there will be a significant disparity in suit lengths. A 6-4 pattern is common:

♠ 9   ♡ K 3   ◇ A J 10 7 5 2   ♣ A K J 3

East assumes West has the minors and bids accordingly. If East bids 5♣ and West removes this to 5◇, expect a freak red two-suiter:

♠ - - -   ♡ K Q J 7 2   ◇ A Q J 6 5 3   ♣ 6 4

Re-open with a double of 4♠ with the red suits if less shapely:

♠ 9   ♡ K Q 7 2   ◇ A Q J 6 5   ♣ K J 8

West	North	East	South
1♣	4♡	4♠	No
4NT ...			

East has bid 4♠ under pressure. Is 4NT Blackwood or does it show the minor two-suiter hand?

(a) ♠ K Q 3   ♡ 6   ◇ K Q 10 2   ♣ A K Q 7 3

(b) ♠ - - -   ♡ 7 2   ◇ K Q J 7 5   ♣ A K 8 6 5 2

With (a), West would want 4NT as Blackwood. With (b), West needs 4NT to show the minors. You really need a bid for each of these hands and the logic of the auction no longer dictates the meaning.

Sometimes it is obvious that 4NT cannot be Blackwood. At other times either interpretation is reasonable. For the sake of uniformity and simplicity, it is reasonable to agree that all non-jump 4NT bids in competition are for takeout. This is also consistent with the principle that finding the right game contract takes precedence over slam bidding in a competitive auction.

This does not mean that you need give up on slam after the above auction with hand (a). You can still bid 4NT. Partner rebids as though you have both minors. When you convert partner's 5♣ or 5◇ to 5♠, this conveys to partner that you had slam interest with the focus being on aces. Partner may be able to judge now whether to pass or whether to push on. Other slam moves are also available, such as 5♡ and 5♠. You and partner simply need to agree on what these would mean.

Sometimes the auction is beyond 4NT already:

West	North	East	South
3♣	3♠	5♣	?

What should South do with this:

♠ K 2   ♡ A J 10 7 4   ◇ A Q J 5 2   ♣ 8

South certainly wants to play in a slam, but the denomination is far from clear. North may have any of these hands:

Chapter 16

Bidding Tactics at Duplicate Pairs

When playing duplicate pairs, part-score contracts are as important as slams because there are the same number of match points at stake on every hand. Almost all part-score results lie between 100 and 200, e.g., 2♠ making = +110, so is 2♣ with an overtrick, 1NT +1 scores 120 and even 2NT +2 scores only 180. Therefore, if your side has the majority of points on a part-score deal a result of +200 will score extremely well, but +100 may leave you with a disappointing score. Playing teams-of-four or rubber bridge you would not risk doubling opponents into game in order to turn +100 into +200, but such tactics are essential at duplicate pairs.

The lure of +200 can tempt you into making some rather dubious penalty doubles. Suppose as North at game all you hold:

♠ 9   ♡ K 8 4 2   ◇ A J 6 3   ♣ J 6 5 2

South opens the bidding with 1♠ and West overcalls with 2♡. You pass for now, but if South re-opens with a double you should pass for penalties. Yes, 2♡ doubled might make, but you have a good defence and a good opening lead, the singleton spade. If you never double the opponents into game at pairs they are getting away with murder.

Note that this risk is far more attractive if your opponents are vulnerable. +200 for one off is likely to be a top score, but +100 if they are not vulnerable will probably not score well. If the opponents are not vulnerable, it is the *second* doubled undertrick (+300 instead of +100) that becomes significant on part-score deals.

If they are vulnerable you should double if you think you have a greater chance of defeating them than they have of making the contract. If they are not vulnerable a good rule of thumb for doubling is that you should believe that you have as good a chance of taking them two off as they have of making it.

All that you have already learned about the need for aggressive protection applies tenfold at duplicate pairs. The following is typical:

Dealer South : Nil vulnerable

```
                   ♠ J 6 5 2
                   ♡ A 8 4 3
                   ◇ J 10 8
                   ♣ Q 5
   ♠ 7 4            N              ♠ K Q 8 3
   ♡ 5                             ♡ 9 7 2
   ◇ A 5 3 2    W       E          ◇ Q 7 4
   ♣ K J 9 6 3 2    S              ♣ A 10 4
                   ♠ A 10 9
                   ♡ K Q J 10 6
                   ◇ K 9 6
                   ♣ 8 7
```

West	North	East	South
			1♡
No	2♡	No	No
3♣	No (1)	No	3♡ (2)
No	No	4♣ (3)	No
No	Dble (4)	All pass	

(1) With a poor ODR North passes, despite the fact that North has four trumps.

(2) These auctions often die at the three-level, usually won by the side with the higher-ranking suit. With a high ODR and a fifth heart, South bids 3♡ in accordance with the LTT. South cannot tell whether either 3♣ or 3♡ or both contracts are making, but 3♡ will be wrong only in the unlikely event that *neither* contract makes.

(3) A typical pairs push, hoping to escape for –100 or less. Note that –100 may score reasonably well even if 3♡ fails because some North-South pairs may have been allowed to play peacefully in 2♡ for 110.

This time there is no doubt. North has enough to defeat 6♥ but it is still foolish to double. If you double and either opponent diagnoses that your double is based on trump winners, there will be a swift flight from 6♥ to 6NT. While you are certain to beat 6♥, there is no certainty that you can take 6NT down. The opponents may have twelve tricks without needing more than two tricks from the hearts.

If you double 6♥ and they run to 6NT making, you have just transformed +50 (or +100 if they are vulnerable) to −990 (or −1440). Who wants that kind of result on their c.v.?

The opponents have landed in a slam where an unlucky trump break will be their downfall. Do not rescue them with an untimely double. Take your profit undoubled and sympathise later with their bad luck. If questioned by partner (who should know better) why you did not double when you had it beaten in your own hand, reply softly, 'But that would have been unsporting, wouldn't it?' Thus you gain a solid reputation as a kindly soul, as well.

While a penalty double of a low-level contract can reap rewards when your opponents have a misfit, once they bid freely to a slam, they have a pretty good idea of their combined assets. Enough said?

For this reason a double of a freely bid slam by the partner of the opening leader is not used on the off-chance that they might have misbid. It is a lead-directing, conventional double, called a *Lightner Double*, after its inventor, Theodore Lightner.

The purpose of this double is not to increase the penalty, but to change the outcome of the deal. It suggests that if partner makes an unexpected lead the slam can be beaten. The thinking goes that if a normal lead is made, the slam is highly likely to succeed, but if partner can be induced to make an unusual lead, the slam will fail. You are thus not trying to increase +50 / +100 to +100 / +200 but to change, say, −980 / −1430 to +50 / +100. Primarily the double asks partner to lead the first suit bid by dummy, not a choice that partner would usually make. It may be that the doubler is void there. Perhaps the doubler is very strong in dummy's suit and fears that declarer's losers there might be discarded unless the suit is led at once.

West	North	East	South
	1♢	2♡	2♠
No	4NT	No	5♡
No	6♣	Double	All pass

What should West lead with these cards after the above auction?

♠ 7 6 2   ♡ Q 8   ♢ Q J 8 7 5 2   ♣ 5 3

Without the double, West would have led the ♡Q with alacrity. The double asks West not to make the natural lead (any suit bid by the defenders or any unbid suit), not to lead a trump but to lead dummy's first bid suit. Chances are that East will ruff the diamond lead and has a trick elsewhere.

What if dummy has not bid a suit, as in this auction:

West	North	East	South
	1NT	No	3♡
No	4♡	No	4NT
No	5♢	No	6♡
No	No	Double	All pass

What should West lead from these hands?

(f)   ♠ 8 5 4   ♡ 7 4 2   ♢ J 10   ♣ 9 6 5 3 2

(g)   ♠ 8 6 4 3   ♡ 7 4 2   ♢ J 10   ♣ 8 6 4 3

(h)   ♠ 8 6   ♡ 7   ♢ 9 7 6 3 2   ♣ 9 7 6 3 2

If partner has a void, where is it likely to be? In the suit where you have most cards. Therefore with (f), you would lead a club.

What if you have equal length in two suits? Sometimes you may have to guess but often there are enough clues. With (g) you should lead a club, not a spade. Given the auction, the opponents may have a 9-card club fit but how could they miss a 9-card spade fit?

With (h), lead a club. If partner wanted a diamond lead, doubling 5♢ was an option. Partner's failure to double 5♢ is clue enough to choose a club rather than a diamond.

A double of a freely bid 3NT contract by the partner of the opening leader is also played as directing.

West	North	East	South
	1♢	No	1♡
1♠	2♢	No	2NT
No	3NT	Double	All pass

If the defenders have bid a suit, the double asks for the lead of that suit. East's double asks West to lead a spade. East is likely to have a top honour doubleton or tripleton.

West	North	East	South
	1♣	1♢	1♡
1♠	2♣	No	2NT
No	3NT	Double	All pass

If both defenders have bid a suit, the double asks for the lead of the suit of the player on lead. The assumption is that without the double West would lead partner's suit. The double asks West to lead a spade.

West	North	East	South
	1♢	No	1♡
No	1♠	No	2NT
No	3NT	Double	All pass

If neither defender has bid a suit, the double asks for the lead of the first suit bid by dummy. Here East is asking for a diamond lead.

West	North	East	South
			1NT
No	3NT	Double	All pass

If no suit has been mentioned, the double announces a solid 5+ suit or K-Q-J-10-x or longer plus an outside ace. East expects to beat 3NT as long as West finds the right suit. Different pairs have different rules. Some play the double as asking for West's shortest suit, even a singleton. A more sensible agreement is for the double to show a solid major, since 3NT denied major suit interest, and ask West to pick the right major. Another option is to be specific: the double of 3NT when no suit has been bid always asks for a spade lead.

Your partner bids a suit and an opponent doubles for penalties. How often are you so confident of success that you want to redouble for business? Not often. Perhaps they have had a massive misunderstanding. Maybe one opponent has doubled for takeout and the other has passed, thinking it was a penalty double. If so, redoubling would be very foolish. It could alert them to their error and allow them to retrieve the situation.

Redouble for business after a penalty double is rarely a wise move. That leaves redouble available for a conventional use. Suppose the bidding has been:

West	North	East	South
	1♠	2♣	No
No	Double	No	No
?			

What should West do with:

♠ 7 6   ♡ Q 9 8 7 5 4   ◇ Q J 9 5 3   ♣ - - -

North has doubled for takeout and South has passed for penalties. It takes little imagination to realise that 2♣ doubled will not be pretty. Your hand is unlikely to bring partner any tricks. Chances are that your side will be much better off playing in a red suit. The S.O.S. redouble asks partner to run from clubs and pick an unbid suit.

Cue-bidding if the opponents have bid two suits

If your opponents have bid one suit, a cue-bid in that suit below 3NT is often used to ask partner for a stopper in their suit. What happens when they have bid two suits?

West	North	East	South	
1◇	1♠	2◇	2♡	It makes sense to play 3♡ as showing a heart stopper and asking for a spade stopper.
3♡ ...				

You could play it the other way around (3♡ asks for a heart stopper) but which agreement does not matter as long as some agreement exists.

(c) ♠ A Q J 9 8 5 ♡ K 5 ◇ K 8 3 ♣ 9 5

(d) ♠ A Q 10 9 5 ♡ K 5 ◇ K 10 7 4 ♣ 9 5

(e) ♠ A Q 10 9 5 ♡ K Q 5 ◇ K 7 6 ♣ 9 5

South bids 5NT over 5♣ to ask North to pick a slam.

With (c) North will choose 6♠ because of quality and length of the spades. South must be prepared for a 6♠ response when bidding 5NT, and so must not bid 5NT with a void or low singleton in spades.

With (d) North is pleased to have a second suit and bids 6◇.

With (e) North should not bid 6♠ even though North has no 4-card red suit. If 6♠ was clearly correct then East would have bid 6♠, not 5NT. North could bid 6◇, but the best action is 6♣ to express doubt. 6♣ says, 'I have no clear action. You choose.' South would then bid 6◇ because of the better suit quality.

South might have bid 6♣ over 5♣ rather than 5NT to ask North to choose a suit. How should 6♣ differ from 5NT? Some might use 6♣ as a grand slam try in spades with first-round club control guaranteed. Another sensible approach is to use 5NT to say, 'I'm playable in three suits' and 6♣ to show a huge two-suiter. For those who play doubles of all pre-empts for takeout and doubles of any immediate raise for takeout, doubling 5♣ adds a further dimension. It is up to you and partner to resolve these dilemmas, preferably before a debacle has made it necessary.

If you bid a suit after 5NT and partner removes that, the inference is that the choice is between the remaining two suits.

WEST	EAST	West	North	East	South
♠ A K 10 4 2	♠ Q 9				3♣
♡ Q 7	♡ A K 8 5 4 3 2	3♠	5♣	5NT	No
◇ K Q 4 3	◇ A 9 7	6◇	No	6♡	No
♣ 7 5	♣ 2	No	No		

6♡ says, 'The choice is hearts or spades, not diamonds.' West is happy to pass 6♡ but with a singleton heart, West would revert to 6♠.

Bids like 5NT or bidding the enemy suit express doubt and imply choice of contracts. In the preceding auction, had East bid 6♦ or 6♥ over 5♣, that would imply a one-suited hand and no spade tolerance.

Unlike many slam conventions which ask questions or tell partner what to do, 4NT and 5NT in competitive auctions ask partner to *co-operate*. Good slam bidding depends as much on judgement as on science.

Lead-Directing Doubles

West	North	East	South	NORTH
1♥	2♣	2♠	No	♠ A 4 2
3♥	No	6♥	No	♥ 7 5 2
No	?			♦ 8
				♣ A Q 10 9 7 3

The opponents bid freely to a slam. You think you have reasonable prospects of beating them because you have two aces and you are on lead. Should you double?

Suppose you double and they do go one off. You have increased the penalty from +50 to +100. Now look at the arithmetic if one of your aces is ruffed. Their score improves from 980 to 1210. Does it make sense to double to gain 50 points at the risk of losing 230? If they redouble, your loss is worse still. They score 1620 if they make it instead of 980. Whether you are playing pairs, teams or rubber bridge, the odds against a speculative double of a slam are huge. At any form of scoring, you will have a great result if the slam is one down undoubled. Be satisfied with that.

Anyway, in the auction given, it is almost certain that your ♣A will not survive. Without the ♠A, East would have used 4NT over 3♥ if East had a club loser as well. The failure to use Blackwood implies that East was not concerned about a possible lack of aces.

West	North	East	South	NORTH
1♥	No	2♠	No	♠ 9 4 3
3♥	No	6♥	No	♥ Q J 10 9
No	?			♦ 8 5
Should North double this time?				♣ Q 10 9 3

120